TRUST ME:
Every Baby Boomer's Nightmare

by Katherine Steel

Copyright © 2013 Alchemy Studios, Inc.

All rights reserved.

ISBN: 978-0-615-81495-7

DEDICATION

To all of the Baby Boomers who are going through, or have gone through family trust nightmares:
I know your pain. GOOD LUCK.
Remember: THIS TOO SHALL PASS.

CONTENTS

	Introduction	1
1	Every Baby Boomer's Nightmare	5
2	The Lights Are On, But Nobody's Home	15
3	I Deserve Everything-I'm The Favorite!	29
4	Vultures In Pinstriped Suits	41
5	Do It Yourself Law If You Can Take It	55
6	Testamentary Capacity	69
7	The Funeral: The Last Stop	77
8	Fallout	85
9	My Lawyer Vs. Your Lawyer	95
10	Trustee, Like It Or Not	107
11	Who Gets What	115
12	Congratulations, You Survived!	125

ACKNOWLEDGMENTS

I'd like to thank all of the crooked attorneys, financial planners, bad caretakers, and most importantly, all of the greedy siblings who have made the stories in this book possible. I couldn't have written it without you.

Introduction

Everyone Wants A Bite Of Your Assets

I wrote this book because I was like a deer in the headlights when I got blindsided by my aging parents, dysfunctional family members, a family trust from hell, and expensive attorneys. I looked all over the internet and bookstores for help, but there was little to no information on the subject except for really dry and boring information written by trust attorneys, who, in some cases, can actually be part of the problem.

When it comes to family money, it's amazing how many vultures come out of the woodwork. It could be "Aunt Icky" and "Uncle Creepy", or the "ever-so-sweet" neighbors that live next door to your aging parents. It could be the phony "do-gooders" who befriend your parents, but in actuality just want a piece of the pie. The worst offenders of all, however, can be STEALING SIBLINGS and DISHONEST TRUST ATTORNEYS who write themselves a giant portion of the trust, cutting you out of your rightful inheritance.

By telling you my stories, and the stories of others, I hope you can avoid the nightmares and pitfalls that happened to me, because they were really hard and expensive lessons to learn. At the time, I found none of what was happening to me TO BE FUNNY…and it really wasn't. But humor is the only way to survive this misery. You may not be able to do anything about your TOXIC FAMILY, but you definitely have some legal rights and options to explore to make things better for you.

This is a "Brave New World" as our generation is just entering the inheritance arena. Mix that with a bad economy, and the situation is ripe for disaster. It is a dog-eat-dog, "Social Darwinism" economic climate right now, and everybody is trolling for money. It's "survival of the fittest": there are no nice guys and no morality, and the most important thing for you to remember is: DON'T EXPECT YOUR SIBLINGS TO BE HONEST OR FAIR. If your family trust has a lawyer written into it, you are probably in DEEP S**T. FORGET THE BANKSTERS: THE TRUST LAWYERS ARE WORSE! These are shark-infested waters and there are little to no roadmaps around. Only one thing is for sure: EVERYBODY WANTS A BITE OF YOUR ASSETS.

There is a WHOLE INDUSTRY based on taking money from your aging parents. The family trust business is a MULTI BILLION DOLLAR industry. Millions are essentially taken from families at the rate of $350 to $500 an hour by unscrupulous attorneys who sometimes even write themselves into trusts as beneficiaries and trustees to control assets that are not theirs. The more dysfunctional the family, the more money they make. They know this. THIS IS THEIR BUSINESS. If you couple this with the onset of Alzheimer's disease, like my father had, then hold onto your seat: they are about to take EVERYTHING.

This book will help to guide you as to what to do and where to go if your family trust struggle isn't over yet, and the FAT LADY HASN'T SUNG. It's going to be hard as hell, BUT YOU CAN WIN. You don't have to sit back and let them take it all. If you have lots of money, then spare yourself the agony: just spend $50,000 or more and let the lawyers take over. But if you're like most of us Americans right now, spending extra money isn't an option. You'll have to do this on your own, and find alternatives that will work.

In this book I will tell you my story and many others, and show you just how you can stop the illegal stealing and BLEEDING of money from your family trust. Just remember that this book is meant to be used as a guideline, and by no means is to be interpreted or used as legal advice. Always consult a professional before you make any decisions. That said, keep in mind that YOU are the one to make the final decisions NO MATTER WHAT.

My hope is that this book will help you navigate through all of the landmines that you may encounter on your journey through FAMILY AND LEGAL HELL. Consider this book as your "don't be an idiot" guide: If you have the stomach for it, TURN THE PAGE AND READ ON.

Chapter One

Every Baby Boomer's Nightmare

Okay, you're reading this book. I can assume at this point that either your aging parents have become a problem, your siblings and/or family suck, you may have a dishonest attorney, a BAD FAMILY TRUST, or all of the above. Does the following sound familiar to you?

The terminally unemployed brother with a family of four? The professional gambler in your family who is always looking for a jackpot? The dysfunctional brother or sister who plays the CRAZY CARD to get what they need? The bipolar "Drama Queen" that threatens suicide, but NEVER GOES THROUGH WITH IT? You know who they are—they're the ones who are always asking for money from your parents. Okay—how about the less obvious ones? The lawyer that befriends your parents in a church or in a temple, portraying him or herself as a good Christian or Jew--someone that you would never think of as anything but trustworthy. Your aging parent's next door neighbor who is always eyeing their antique furniture. The Filipino caretaker that comes in at the end to take care of your parents. The realtor that is trying to get your parents to sell their house to his friend for nothing. The list is never-ending. These people could turn out to be predators. Many of them conduct their predatory businesses through churches, temples, and even charities, taking their unsuspecting and vulnerable victims off guard. You might hear your parent say more than once:

> "Why Dan is such a kind man--he's a trust attorney and will do our Family Trust for a VERY REASONABLE price. He would never do anything DISHONEST. I see him at church every Sunday".

These predators have it down. They tell your parents that they aren't going to charge much because "WE'RE FRIENDS". Your parents are thrilled because it doesn't cost them much up front, but don't worry: the attorneys will make it up by the bucket-load in the end, as they sometimes write themselves in as either trustees or beneficiaries, and are able to charge outrageous fees to the unsuspecting heirs. But after all, THEY'RE FRIENDS, AND THEY GO TO THE SAME CHURCH.

Your dysfunctional brother or sister are also pros as well at this game. They have done this their whole lives, they know what works, and they have refined it to a "T". You know the rap; they tell your parents:

"I can't pay my bills, I need a loan."

"I need to go to rehab."

"The job is coming-they're calling me next week."

"I need to retrain-can you pay for it? I promise I'll pay you back."

"What will happen to us and the grandkids if you don't loan us money? We'll be out on the streets!"

"I need to borrow some more money just this one last time."

The problem with the "JUST THIS ONE LAST TIME" is that it can last FOREVER.

It's family blackmail, pure and simple. What's worse is that the blackmailing sibling feels entitled to it. They know exactly how to press your parent's cash machine buttons. To them, your parents are an endless twenty-four hour ATM, always open to hear their tales of woe, and to dispense cash to make them feel better.

Your aging parents justify your sibling's behavior to you, and the dialogue may sound like this:

"Tom is really trying. He's been sober now for over a month."

"It's not really her, it's that damn husband of hers. We can't let her go hungry!"

"You know your brother. He's not like you. He just

can't handle his finances. He's never been as good with money as you."

You hear all of this, and it's so upsetting to you that either you don't deal with it, or you try and reason with your sibling about it, to no avail of course. You might even tell your parents to cut the purse strings, but the dysfunctional relationship just keeps going. That was the case with my brother. He played the part of the "poor dysfunctional guy who just couldn't cope with life", so my dad had to support his family for fifteen years. My brother didn't even have to grovel for the money. He made the "Poor pathetic me" phone call to my parents once a month starting the conversation in his best "Eddie Haskell" voice: "How are you doing? Hope all is well", acting as though he was really interested in them. NOT! He would then spin his tale of woe: his struggle with alcoholism, his futile search for employment, and when the phone call would get to the end, he would say in a joking voice "What's a phone call from me without a pitch for money?" Sometimes my dad would send him a check to pay the mortgage, my brother would cash it, and spend the money on other things. My dad finally started paying the mortgage directly to the bank after my brother was an inch away from foreclosure for month after month. After that, my brother didn't even worry about the mortgage anymore. He would call for money FOR OTHER THINGS!

My dad used to tell me all of this, and I'd tell him to cut my brother off, and let him figure his money problems out on his own. All of us have to work, and just about everyone has rent, mortgage, and bills to pay. My brother's attitude was like that joke:

> "I've been told that working won't kill me, but why take that chance?"

A job, ANY kind of job would have done him good. At least he wouldn't have been focusing on himself all day. It didn't dawn on me at the time that my brother was single-handedly WIPING OUT MY PARENTS ASSETS. He had taken the "retire by groveling" road, and the situation had taken on the speed of a locomotive. As my parents got older, there was no stopping the train; my brother had weaseled over three hundred thousand dollars worth of "I NEED MONEY JUST ONE LAST TIME". "Wow, what a terrible person!" You might think. "What a selfish individual he was for trying to sponge every dime out of his aging parents!" Not an isolated incident, I've found out. As a matter of fact, even U.S. President James Madison and his wife Dolly lost the entire estate of Montpelier because they had to pay all of the gambling debts and high interest loans that their son Payne had accrued over the years. President Madison wrote letter after letter pleading with him to stop borrowing money and to stop spending wildly, but to no avail. After President Madison died, his wife Dolly was left penniless due to her son's debts.

The more I talked to people about my situation, the more I realized that just about every family had a nightmare. A friend told me about her brother, "Dwayne". He was "the ever-so-caring brother who's sacrificed everything to take care of his mother by staying with her". WRONG! He moved himself and his family in because he had no job and nowhere else to go. Once there, he quickly started liquidating all of her assets, unbeknownst to his siblings. He even asked them for money to "take care of Mom". He bought things for her that she "needed": A big screen TV. A state-of-the-art stereo. And to drive her to the doctor's office: A ROLLS ROYCE! Suspicions arose in the family after THAT purchase, but still no one bothered to question him. They would even visit the house where their mother would sit alone in her self-sufficient bedroom that she never left, still not questioning their brother's behavior. No one wanted to deal with the problems that stood right in front of their eyes. Ever on the make for "money for Mom", Dwayne would always have his hand out for more donations at family functions. When the mother finally died, there was no money left in her estate for her funeral. Actually, there was no money left for ANYTHING. Dwayne had taken mortgages and credit cards out in his mother's name and liquidated everything. The Rolls was repossessed, as was the house. After all of this, his wife left him, and he moved to Vegas. Undaunted, he still kept asking for donations. After all, he was the "the ever-so-caring brother who's sacrificed everything to take care of his mother by staying with her". Once the mother was gone, he lost his "benefactors". They were done with him. He ended up dying of a heart attack in Vegas, penniless and alone...no one left to leech from. This situation is really common in families. He made it too easy for everyone by moving in with his mother and taking care of her, and in the long run everyone in the family suffered for it.

The problem is that most of us are just too busy to deal with our aging parents. Keeping up a job, a house, and a family is full time work, and finding time to visit your parents usually is somewhere on the bottom of the list. Sad fact, but true for most. The person that has the most time on their hands is the unemployed loser sibling that is going to visit them to ask for more money, anyway. The parents, who are elderly and desperate for ANY kind of attention, as they mostly sit in their houses and listen to their brains bounce around the walls, or worst yet, sit in the house and watch a steady feed of FOX NEWS and are terrified to leave their homes, are happy to see ANYBODY. This dysfunctional relationship works this way: the parents still feel needed, and the SIBLING is happy that he or she doesn't have to GET A JOB! I have a friend whose sister moved in with his aging father, had him put her name on all of the checking accounts and the title of the house, then PUT HIM INTO A HOME! My friend found out about it, then hired an attorney. He went with the attorney to the home, had his dad sign a power of attorney, then got him out of the place. My friend then moved his dad into his own home, and used the power of attorney to get his father back possession of the house and his money. His sister still went through a lot of his father's assets, but at least he was able to stop the FINANCIAL BLEEDING.

This kind of behavior—the idea that one sibling deserves everything because they are the "favorite", is devastating to other family members, and the incredible thing is that the "favorite" sibling feels totally justified in TAKING EVERYTHING. Most don't have a shred of guilt. A friend of mine's mother had so convinced her father that her sister didn't care for him that he transferred all of his money into her accounts, and left the sister an insulting sum when he died, EVEN THOUGH SHE HAD MADE A POINT OF

VISITING HIM, AND CALLING HIM ONCE A WEEK. This was the last "F**k you!" so to speak. Great way to be remembered by your ancestors. Of course, the sister never spoke to the mother again, and the mother wrote off her sister's relationship for a couple hundred thousand bucks. She still feels that she was right in doing so.

Sometimes it's the kids who screw their parents in inheritance issues. When my uncle died, his portion of a family property went directly to his kids, bypassing his wife, who was broke. She asked her kids for a portion of it so that she could survive, and they said NO. Ouch. When it comes to inheriting money, THE GLOVES ARE OFF. The "Reptilian" behavior comes out. The only safety net that we can create so that these things don't happen to us is planning our inheritances with our parents. Getting them to open up about it. Getting them to DEAL with what happens to their family when they die.

What happens to most of us is that when we start to notice our parents going downhill, we don't really accept, or want to deal with the ramifications of it. My friend Victor noticed that his dad was starting to forget to pay his bills, and had lost track of the balances in his business accounts. He took his dad to the doctor, who diagnosed him with dementia. As Victor was executor of the family trust, he decided that he should look at the books at his father's business, and see where all of the money was going. The business was an international company that made shirts for boutiques all around the world. Victor's dad's partner was Victor's brother in law, who did all of the traveling around the world to promote the business. When Victor did a forensic audit, he found huge sums of money missing from the accounts. Upon further investigation, he found out that the Brother-In Law was using the money to spend on girlfriends that he had in different countries! Victor didn't know how to tell his sister without hurting her, but he felt that she had to know. When she found out, she not only got a divorce, it created a family s**t storm of epic proportions when the other siblings had found out that her husband had stolen all of their inheritance. Multiple lawsuits against each other tore the family to shreds.

If your parents are reaching the age where they are starting to lose it and need help with their finances, get involved with their problems before someone less scrupulous than you does.

Chapter Two

The Lights Are On, But Nobody's Home

My real journey through this nightmare started when my dad was diagnosed with dementia. How did I find out about it? MY BROTHER WAS UPSET THAT MY DAD HAD MISSED PAYING HIS MORTGAGE! Since my dad had always paid my brother's mortgage directly to the bank, the bank had notified my brother of the non-payment. This obviously frightened my brother on many levels, as his mortgage wasn't the only thing that my dad was paying for: he was paying for everything! Concerned that "The Bank of Bob" (my dad) suddenly was having some accounting problems, he wrote an email to my father's attorney and demanded that the payments continue:

To: Katherine Steel, Dick Richards, Esq.

Subject: The Time Has Come

Katherine and Dick,

I'm bringing up a sensitive issue here, but the TIME HAS COME to talk about it. As you probably have now found out, Dad has been paying my mortgage for me for quite some time now until I can find a job and get back on my feet. As Katherine has seen first hand, Dad's handling of money has been erratic, to say the least. Apparently, while he was preparing for his trip with Aunt Deedee, he failed to pay my mortgage payment, something that he had never done before. I dare say that his mind might be failing him at this point.

I'm sending this email to both of you to make you aware that I want to be completely on the up and up to both of you about this. It seems to me that the best solution for us temporarily is to have Dick's office issue a check to my mortgage company. The amount paid to me from the Trust will obviously be deducted from my share of the inheritance. What I need now is an agreement from both of you on how to proceed with letting Dad know that he missed the payment, and letting him know that Dick's office should handle the payments from now on, since he can't be depended upon to write the checks. My mortgage is only six days late, so we still have time to make the payment, if we do it ASAP. On another subject, my daughter needs $4000 for the first payment of Cosmetology School, which is due this month, and my car payment is way overdue on my Ford Focus. Please let me know when I will be receiving the check for my mortgage and the check for my daughter's tuition. I'll talk to the car finance company and see if I can hold them off for a while longer. Thank you both for bearing with me during these hard times.

Sincerely,

Robbie Steel Jr.

What else can be said about an email like this? "Paying his mortgage for some time"—try FIFTEEN YEARS. "Getting back on his feet"—NEVER. The fake sincerity about my father's dementia: GIVE ME A BREAK. His only concern and reaction to my father losing his mind was that his mortgage and daughter's tuition wasn't being paid. He also passive aggressively included his car payment so that we might give him some money for that, too. Now that my father was out of the picture, he had selected the lawyer and I to be his new benefactors.

I was so pissed by the attitude of entitlement of the letter that it made me make up some of my own lyrics to the tune of the "Beverly Hillbillies":

"Let me tell you the story of a man named Bob,

He had a son that wouldn't get a job,

He gave him all his money and the other kid got pissed,

And now that he's gone all the money will be missed!"

It would be a lot funnier if it wasn't true. If I didn't make up stupid songs and make jokes about the situation while it was happening, I would have lost my mind by now.

The next part of this dementia drama was convincing my dad to leave his home and get into a retirement village. A World War II Marine Veteran doesn't listen to, or respect, anybody, so he decided to find a place himself. He got on this kick how "Sunrise Village" was the place to be. After all, they had called him on the phone, and they were SO NICE. They would even make arrangements to pick him up. HOW SWEET OF THEM!

So we picked up my dad and went to Sunrise Village, a new retirement development in the middle of nowhere. The sales reps are hired to look especially dowdy. You know the type—she wore stretch pants in a lavender color with a floral printed blouse. She also had a little gold necklace with a cross, just to give the outfit a sense of sincerity. Her hair was a "bubble" look: curly with a nondescript color. "Susie" led us into an office where we could look at all of the posters of happy seniors playing golf, cards, shuffleboard, and by the pool. All of the photography had been softened to give it a nice, glowing, happy look. Susie sweetly asked us about our family, with a smile that told us that she had heard it all a hundred times and didn't give a crap.

We got into her golf cart, and she showed us the place: aside from an old guy in a walker desperately trying to make it up a hill, it was empty. It was untouched. Never lived in. We saw the pool with nobody in it. There was one old lady in the dining room having a cup of Sanka. We looked at the "model" apartments, and, of course, my dad wanted the biggest. It was a big, dusty, empty unit that looked like it had been sitting for a while. She then took us back to her office for the kill. Susie sat us all down and laid the price on us: $680,000 in escrow, $5,000 a month! Susie then talked smoothly through the loud GASP she had just heard from all of us, "Of course, the $680,000 will be refunded when the unit is sold again, and they're selling like hotcakes!" Right. What a bargain: $680,000! After all, the retirement community was in the middle of butthole nowhere. Damn! Sign me up now! But wait-- the best is yet to come! The company that owned the place was a Limited Liability Corporation out of Delaware. You know, the state aside from Florida where you have no accountability, and bankruptcy is the norm? And, when you want to sell the place, you have to wait until they get a buyer for your apartment. YEAH, RIGHT, WHEN PIGS FLY. I told this to my dad's lawyer, thinking that he'd agree that the place was a rip-off. Instead, he answered "Susie is a heck of gal, and what's more, your dad wants to put down a $68,000 deposit on it."

The sickeningly sweet Susie the Saleswoman had just become the latest in the group of vultures circling the estate. Coupled with my father's crooked attorney, my father's trust money was about to vanish like a Houdini act. Little did the two vultures know, my dad had no idea that the price was $680,000. He thought it was $68,000! Okay. The brain had left the dock, and was floating in the sea without a paddle. The lights were on but nobody was home. Susie, and my dad's lawyer, made sure that the deal was moving through. However, my dad needed to be evaluated and signed off for independent living. His personal physician gave him a test. Guess what? HE DIDN'T PASS IT! Not exactly breaking news to me, but he was diagnosed with dementia, and would require assisted living. My dad accused the doctor of lying. "I'm not demented!" he kept saying over and over. The more angry he got about it, the more demented he sounded. It was pretty ugly.

After hearing this, Susie the Saleswoman freaked out. After all, she wanted her commission. She had spent many hours with my dad and she wanted the big $680,000 payoff. She called me and asked me to have the doctor remove the "x" that he had made on the dementia diagnosis, and say instead that my father had mild senility, so he would be eligible for Sunrise Village! I said

"SORRY SUSIE, I DON'T THINK SO, THE DEAL IS OFF. I'LL HAVE TO FIND A PLACE WITH ASSISTED LIVING THAT'S CHEAPER THAN THE FACILITIES YOU'RE OFFERING!"

I quickly called Dick the Lawyer, and told him to cancel the $68,000 deposit that we gave them. When that happened, Sweet Susie turned into SCARY SUSIE! She kept calling me like a stalker. I felt like Michael Douglas in "Fatal Attraction"—Scary Susie was not going to let the deal die. Eventually the calls stopped. She must have found fresh blood from another desperate family. Poor bastards.

Being old and demented and by yourself is not a pretty picture. You are like the old fisherman in Hemingway's book "The Old Man and the Sea"; everyone wants to take a bite out of the big fish you've caught until the only things that are left when you get to the dock are the bones. You are a sitting duck for all sorts of scams: sometimes it can be your next door neighbor that's trying to put one over on you! I have one piece of advice when it comes to dealing with your parent's creepy neighbors: WHENEVER YOU NOTICE A BOOK OF PRAYING HANDS ON A COFFEE TABLE, RUN AS FAR, AND AS FAST AS YOU CAN!

These people disguise themselves as kind, caring Christians, when in actuality they are BLOOD SUCKING SCUM. BEWARE OF THE RELIGIOUS LINGO: THEY ARE OUT FOR ANYTHING THEY CAN GET THEIR GREEDY PAWS ON, AND ARE USING THE BIBLE TO JUSTIFY IT!

At least this was the case with my father's creepy neighbor who wanted to be his REALTOR. Mind you, he wasn't a realtor at all, but an attorney who wanted to get into the real estate business by selling my dad's house. He and his wife Tammy used all of the Christian tactics they could: they took my dad to church, gave him sculptures with praying hands, watched "700 Club" specials with him on TV, and gave him religious DVDs. Mind you, religion was never my dad's priority when I was a kid, as he was too busy at the "Church of the 18 hole Golf Course" on Sundays. Now that he was getting older, he decided to invest some time to hedge his bet on going to heaven (upstairs) or hell (downstairs). Personally, I was betting on him getting an asbestos suit for all of his bad doings, and didn't believe that a bad sculpture of some praying hands was going to get him into the "going up" elevator.

My first contact with my dad's creepy neighbors was when they came running wildly out of their house to ask us to have a friendly cup of coffee. The "creep-o-meter" pinned itself to maximum immediately. They were so sickeningly sweet they reminded me of something—I got it—"Seven-up" mixed with Fleet's Phosphate Soda. I instantly felt like I was prepping for a colonoscopy and was about to get reamed. They were pressuring my dad to list his home with them, and they weren't even realtors! This courting went on for months. At this point my dad's brain, remember, had left the dock and was floating in dangerous seas. I called my dad's attorney voicing my concerns and objections to my father entering into a contract with them. SURPRISE! He was friends with the neighbor! They played golf with each other on occasion, and belonged to the same country club! Sound fishy? My gut feeling from this statement was that this was going to be a REALLY, REALLY, BAD deal my father was getting into.

Now I had to battle three vultures: My brother, my father's attorney….and the "realtor". Against all of my arguments and concerns, they went ahead and signed papers with the creepy realtor. I voiced my disapproval through this email:

Dear Jim and Tammy,

My father cannot balance a checkbook, and cannot pay his bills on his own. Nor can he fill out a check. He also has trouble differentiating between twenty five hundred dollars, and two and a half million dollars.
For several years, bank tellers were balancing his checkbook for him, until his lawyer, Dick, took over all financial transactions for him. It even got so bad that Dick advised my brother to take away his checkbook. Now my dad carries around small amounts of cash that Dick gives him, and hopes that whoever he gives it to

will give him the correct change. I was so concerned about my dad's financial incompetence and Dick's complete power over his transactions that I contacted Adult Protective Services, who did an independent financial competency test by a Psychiatrist, which my father failed. That was two years ago. I insist that my father be evaluated for financial competency with an impartial psychiatrist by the State before you proceed on the sale of his house. I can supply you and Dick with all of the information on who to contact at Adult Protective Services, who are aware of the case. It would remove any doubt from any party, and would be the most honest and forthright way of handling Dad's estate.

Sincerely,
Katherine Steel

Of course, they did not want to hear any of this, as they had their eyes set on getting a big bite out of the Steel family pie. They told my father about my letter, and things got even worse. My father signed with them to sell the home, and was angry with me for questioning his decision. Of course, he forgot what he was angry about five minutes later!

They decided to spend more of my dad's money for an unnecessary STAGING OF THE HOME. They placed artificial flowers, crosses, and Christian knick knacks everywhere, and painted one of the rooms pink. The place looked like a Tijuana whorehouse when they were done with it, and the Trust paid $12,000 for it! I was outraged, and questioned the bill, for I saw nothing that added up to that amount. Tammy, the creepy realtor neighbor's wife, was offended by my comments, and her husband replied that "She was hurt after all her hard work to create a beautiful environment". Beautiful if you're on acid. What a nightmare!

So I was battling three vultures, but I didn't see this one coming:

THE SLEAZY SISTER IN LAW!

I always wondered about my Aunt Deedee. As a matter of fact, the whole family wondered about her. She was a bitter school teacher that always sent each of us a stale fruit basket at Christmas. The dynamics at the Christmas dinner table were always intense when she was there. Lifetime schoolteachers are used to telling kids what to do, and they usually talk to adults in the same fashion. She was very argumentative, and judgmental, to say the least, which didn't coincide with her pretentious Christian "better than thou" philosophy. She also had a dog, her surrogate child, that was scared of linoleum floors. Even though she didn't have any kids of her own, she always criticized my mother on how she was raising us.

Fast forward to my mother's last days. In comes my weird aunt, out of the blue, who then moved in with my father. Then they put my mom into a rest home that resembled "The Snake Pit"! They did it because "It would be too much for your father to keep her at home". My mother died a horrible, sad, lonely death in the place, and the next thing that happened was really toxic: my sleazy aunt and NOW my sleazy dad went on a cruise to Europe together! When they came back, she moved in with him....of course, for his WELL BEING. She quickly took on my mom's roles, even to the last detail of wearing my mom's pink velour jumpsuit and jade jewelry. When I was visiting them once, I noticed a picture of her wearing my mom's mink coat on my dad's desk....at first I thought it was a picture of a gerbil. Unfortunately, it was her: she was never a looker, that's for sure.

But wait...there's more. She befriended all of my father's neighbors, and decided that she was now playing the role of my mother. She would call me and give me "advice" about what to do with my father. Instead of being weird and eccentric, she was now weird, eccentric, and OBNOXIOUS! I began to feel like I was watching "Sunset Boulevard" and was waiting for the monkey scene. I think she, too, was waiting for her close-up....which never came, especially after my father died. Her delusions of grandeur disintegrated in one fell swoop. No more pretending to be the woman of the house, no more vacations, and worst of all: NO MONEY LEFT FOR AUNT DEEDEE IN THE TRUST. Not even enough for a dry cleaning bill for the pink jumpsuits and a box of depends. She also found out the hard way that my father was one of those kind of guys that would step on your head to save himself from a flood, and that was just what he did to her.

Let's see, sleazy siblings, rotten relatives, and creepy neighbors. How about nieces and nephews? My friend Ray's parents both got dementia at the same time. Hell on earth. Wouldn't wish it on my worst enemy. Since he lived in LA, and they lived in New Jersey, he had to commute on weekends to take care of their affairs. His niece volunteered to look in on them everyday and also to grocery shop for them. She only lived a few blocks away. Ray was charmed by his generous niece, and gave her a weekly salary to help out. Feeling that his parents were in good hands, he continued his life in Los Angeles, without the grueling weekend commute to New Jersey. He called his niece and parents every other day just to make sure that things were going well. Months went by, and everything seemed okay. WRONG. He had forwarded all of his parent's bills to his home, and every month paid the phone bill, the utilities, et cetera, until he came across a credit card bill. He almost had a heart attack when he saw the bill for thirty thousand dollars of stereos, TVs, clothes, car repairs, jewelry, restaurants, you name it: it was on there. He called the credit card company and said "This has to be some kind of mistake—my parents are invalids and sit in front of the TV all day—they don't even have a car! This has to be a case of identity theft!" The credit card company informed that they would look into it, and get back to him. In the meantime, they would put a freeze on the credit card.

He didn't mention it to his parents, as he didn't want them to get upset. A few days later, he got a phone call from his niece claiming that she couldn't buy groceries the other day for his parents because the credit card account was frozen. Ray replied that he froze it because "Some a**hole must have stolen the numbers and was on a spending spree all over New Jersey". Dead silence on the other end. Ray asked if she was still there. She told him that she had to go, and would talk to him later. Not thinking anything of it, he hung up the phone and went back to his life. A few days later, he found out from the credit card company that it was his niece and her boyfriend who went on the spending spree. Ray called her and let her have it. He told her to return everything, and pay him back, as his parents were broke and Ray was barely making ends meet. She told him to f**k himself, and that she deserved everything she had bought because she was taking care of his parents and he wasn't paying enough. After she hung up, Ray did something that most family members would never do. He called the police and told them that his niece and boyfriend had stolen his parent's credit cards, and had charged $30,000 without permission.

Talk about a family war. This was Hiroshima. The police arrested his niece and her boyfriend, the rest of Ray's family hated him for it, and when the niece and boyfriend got out of jail, they plastered his picture all over the internet calling him a "faggot"!

Moral of the story: nothing is "free". Especially from family members. Or how about non-family members: the hired "caretaker"?

The Bradleys could no longer care for themselves because of advanced forms of dementia and their family hired Norma Cheesman to be a live-in caregiver. What no one knew about Norma was that she was a seasoned predator with a plan. This was not Norma's first rodeo as a caretaker. She had lassoed many a doggie, and now she had hit the mother lode with Caroline's parents. In 10 months she made Caroline's parents homeless and penniless. How did she do it? She literally grabbed Caroline's father's hand, and made him sign on the dotted line, giving her power of attorney, naming her as beneficiary of his estate, and what's worse: disinheriting his wife! She forced Caroline's demented father into signing a reverse mortgage on the house which was free and clear of debt, and the money he received from the reverse mortgage she put into her own account. Then she had Caroline's father withdraw huge amounts of cash from the couple's savings and persuaded him to buy the home that she was living in. One thing's for sure, you can't call Cheesman "cheesy"--this was GRAND LARCENY. In the end, the family lost more than $300,000, AND their parent's home. By the time Cheesman was done, there was only $374 left in their account! All of this happened under Caroline's nose, because she visited them all of the time, and suspected nothing. "I called my mom and dad every single day." Caroline said. "It's not like we weren't involved with my parents. But she pulled the wool over our eyes and was methodical in taking every single penny that she could." Cheesman is on the lam, nowhere to be found, and poor Caroline didn't inherit anything but misery. The lesson: CHOOSE YOUR HELP WISELY.

The biggest lesson from all of these stories is that it is IMPERATIVE to discuss your parent's assets and financial issues BEFORE THEY BECOME DEMENTED. I know a family that has a meeting once a month with all family members to air their grievances and concerns regarding family money and trust issues. It's best to know where everything is, and where everybody stands before dementia descends upon your family. Most important: NO SECRETS: Everything needs to be vetted.

Chapter Three

"I Deserve Everything: I'm The Favorite!"

Face it: are you really surprised by your brother or sister's attitude that "they deserve everything"? Are you really in that much denial? WAKE UP! They've probably been a**holes your WHOLE LIFE! If they are older than you, it probably all started when they were the only child and along came the new brother or sister (you), thus ruining all of the attention that they were getting from your parents. No longer were they the center of attention. Now mommy and daddy were paying a lot of attention to the newborn, and a lifelong jealousy was created. They may have even been tormenting you behind your parent's back. REMEMBER? Or it could be the other way around. You could be the successful older brother or sister, or more attractive brother or sister that your parents always doted on, creating jealousy that way. All of this could have started in any number of ways. It could have been the pony ride that you went on without them. Or the fact that the clown gave you a better present than your sibling at the birthday party. These little murders have gone on and on throughout your entire life, through high school, college, marriage, et cetera. The jealousies have kept growing until now they are a huge festering boil waiting to explode. A friend of mine told me, "People change—but not that MUCH". It's true. Some people get past all of the hurts and inequities of childhood and move on. Some people still hold onto the crap. IT KEEPS THEM GOING. It's what they live for. The "I deserve everything sibling" has a belief that they are ENTITLED TO IT ALL. When the parents are gone, they will get everything because THEY WERE THE UNDERDOG, AND DAD WAS ALWAYS FOR THE UNDERDOG! I mean, they really weaseled money and manipulated your parents and others all of their lives, but in their own demented minds, they're the UNDERDOG and they should receive everything. It doesn't matter that you worked your ass off for your whole life to get your own money, they feel like they deserve it, too. A whole lot of RATIONALIZATION going on, and next to impossible to reason with. In either situation, your sibling always wanted the attention, and never got the kind that they wanted. Now that the parents are gone, they are out for blood—YOURS.

In this chapter, I discuss various personality disorders and how they affect everyone living in the family. Think about it for a second. Your sibling is trying to screw you out of your inheritance. Where is this coming from? "Gee, why is Robbie such a PRICK?" If you remember, Robbie was always a prick. He dropped you in the middle of nowhere, in the pouring rain, just so he could be alone with his girlfriend. REMEMBER? PRICK! Or how about Candy, your sister, who stole from your parent's checking account while you were living in Oregon and blamed you for it, even though you hadn't been to San Francisco the whole year? REMEMBER? A**HOLE!

"NO BRAINER" HERE…. family dysfunction is the biggest cause of inheritance wars. Death always brings the vultures out. It's the smell of blood, or, excuse me, money. However your parents decided to divide the estate, you and your siblings will take this as the final statement of what they thought of you. Even though it may just be a screwed-up document that was poorly drafted, this last statement reverberates to your very core the resentments, entitlements, and downright nasty sibling rivalry you may have had. Even if your parents tell you that they love you on their deathbed, if you don't end up getting the gold watch or the car or whatever you always wanted from them, you're going to feel betrayed for the rest of your life. Your parent's lives, in the end, have been boiled down to a legal document that dictates what they thought of you. Maybe they thought you were worth a house, maybe a car….or maybe just an old sofa and a bottle of aspirin!

Sometimes there is a sibling that is overcompensating late in your parent's life, hoping that they'll get it all if they put in the effort the last few years. It happens all the time. My brother feels absolutely entitled to the $300,000 my parents gave to support him for many years just because he was around the final few years of my dad's life. I know that deep down he resented my dad. My dad always insulted him, called him fat, and ordered him around. Maybe he felt entitled to the money because of all the insults he had to endure from him. The family dynamics and personality disorders all come out of the closet when the last parent dies. I'm a great example myself: I'm writing this book because of all of the unfinished business I have with my parents.

Below is a list of personality disorders. See which one your siblings, or family members fit into:

According to Joseph M. Carver, Phd, a clinical psychologist, personality disorders are divided into three groups of "clusters".

- Cluster A personality disorders are individuals who have odd, eccentric behaviors. Paranoid, Schizoid, and Schizotypal Personalities fall into this cluster.
- Cluster B are personalities that are highly dramatic, both emotionally and behaviorally. Antisocial, Borderline, Narcissistic, and Histrionic Personality are in this group.
- Cluster C are personalities characterized by being anxious and fearful. Avoidant, Dependent, and Obsessive-Compulsive Personality fall into this cluster.

In the general population, the largest number of personality disorders fall into the Cluster B group, which we will discuss in this chapter. The four personality disorders in Cluster B are:

Antisocial Personality – ranges from individuals who are chronically irresponsible, unsupportive con-artists to those who have total disregard for the rights of others and commit criminal acts with no remorse.

They are known for treating people terribly, wiping out checking accounts, credit cards and the theft of family items. People with this disorder tend to lie or steal and often fail to fulfill jobs or parenting responsibilities. The terms "sociopath" and "psychopath" are sometimes used to describe a person with antisocial personality disorder. SOUND FAMILIAR? These two charming brothers are a good example of anti-social behavior:

The brothers, both in their 50s, lived rent-free in their father's home. During the time that they were living there, they allowed their 86 year old father to waste away malnourished, dehydrated, and caked in filth. Prosecutors alleged that the brothers refused to provide proper care to their father so that they could inherit all of their parent's savings. One of their relatives blew the whistle on their scheme. One day on a visit, they found the father in only a T-shirt and socks. One sock had grown into his feet, as the elderly father had been wearing the bloodied, feces-covered socks for at least a year. At the hospital, a doctor found that his feet were rotting, along with suffering an array of other life-threatening ailments.

A social service worker visited the brothers, responding to the troublesome report from the hospital visit. Despite the fact that the father had large savings, enough to pay for his care, one brother said that they thought about it, but thought that it was better for the family to take care of him other than strangers!

Not exactly a warm and caring son, but he did have a point. Sometimes having a caregiver taking care of your parents can be even worse! But how would you know if you weren't around? A daughter who suspected foul play after several of her mother's teeth were missing put hidden surveillance cameras in her invalid mother's bedroom to see if everything was on the up and up with the caretaker that she had hired. The caretaker, oblivious to the cameras, was videotaped pushing the mother into her bed, shoving her, and slapping her. Unfortunately, there weren't any cameras in the bathroom that night, because the caretaker put her mother into scalding hot bathwater, causing second degree burns. Not exactly Florence Nightingale!

Here's another example of an antisocial son and father relationship. It was 39 degrees outside when the son pulled his car over along the highway and put his 92-year-old father on the margin in the middle of nowhere, leaving him lying there. His father couldn't walk without his walker, and his son knew it. The son, who had a drinking problem (you think?), told police "I tried to kill my father. I'm sorry." Horrible sounding, isn't it? You ever think that maybe his father drove him to drinking? We'll never know, because a grand jury indicted him on charges of endangerment and aggravated assault.

A psychopath falls under the heading of antisocial behavior, also. The psychopath is either unable or unwilling to control their impulses or to delay gratification. They use their rage to control people and manipulate them into submission. Like these caregivers from a rest home in Germany: one caregiver was caught attempting to perform surgery on a dying patient without using any anesthesia. He also gave an overdose of morphine to another patient that led to their death. In the same rest home, another caregiver was caught removing a resident's breathing tube and mocking him by asking how it felt to have no air! Let's hope people in Germany aren't lining up to get into that place.

Borderline Personality – Common characteristics include panic, fears of abandonment, unstable social relationships, unstable self-image, self-damaging acts such as promiscuity, substance abuse, alcohol use, recurrent suicide thoughts and attempts, self-injury and self-mutilation.

Either you have one in your family, or you know of one in a friend's family. This is the sibling that will do anything to get attention. They will use heroin addiction, alcoholism, or even suicide to get attention. A friend of mine had been saving many years for his daughter's college education only to spend it on a rehab hospital because she couldn't stay away from heroin, and the death/rescue cycle that she had created with her parents. He would bail her out of jail, she would promise not to do drugs, and then it would start all over again. It's the constant threat to the parent—if you don't pay attention to me, give me money, etc., I can't guarantee that something BAD WON'T HAPPEN TO ME. I know this type well—my brother used it on my dad for fifteen years. Funny thing. NOTHING BAD EVER HAPPENED TO HIM! My brother used to play my parents for money with dramatic weird letters like this one to them:

Dear Mom and Dad,

I'm sorry for the financial pain that my situation continues to cause you, but the only person who is really suffering is *ME*. My alcoholism is a monkey on my back that I can't get rid of. I drink because I need to blot out my feelings of inadequacy. I've learned now that feelings are valuable tools for living, and they tell you when something's wrong. Like *Jiminy Cricket said*: without them, you're playing a guessing game. I have no idea how to make amends to you for the past ten years of my life, but God willing, I'll find a way to do it financially.

Love,

Robbie Jr.

Letters like these take manipulating one's parents to a new level, and it worked on my parents, who worried constantly about him. My brother, in these weird letters, also diffused my dad's bad temper by INSULTING HIMSELF before my dad could get to it. This relationship is an example of the classic rescue/rescuer cycle, and it really cried out for a family intervention, but neither my dad nor my brother would have it.

Histrionic Personality – a pervasive pattern of excessive emotional display and attention-seeking. Individuals with this personality are excessively dramatic and are often viewed by the public as the "Drama Queen" type of individual. They are often sexually seductive and highly manipulative in relationships.

The best examples of this are the women or men that come in for the kill when they meet someone who has recently been widowed and is lonely. It's like the Anna Nicole Smith story--the famous "Black Widow" so to speak, who makes a sad, lonely man sexually active and happy again, and then gets him to sign over every last dime to her before he dies, cheating the family members of their inheritances.

Robert Ludlum, the famous novelist who wrote "The Bourne Identity" and many other great thrillers, died from burns from a fire that started in his house from unknown causes. According to his nephew and biographer, Dr. Kenneth Michael Kearns, when the fire department arrived at the scene they found Ludlum in a burning chair screaming and on fire. In the kitchen, firefighters found Ludlum's second wife Karen belligerent and uncooperative. "F**k off", she told them "I'm fixing myself a drink". She refused to accompany her husband to the hospital in the ambulance. In Kearns biography entitled "The Ludlum Identity" he states that Ludlum had changed his will to the financial benefit of his second wife weeks before his death. There now is an investigation into whether it was foul play or not. Whatever it was, it doesn't sound like it was a marriage made in heaven.

Narcissistic Personality – a pervasive preoccupation with admiration, entitlement, and egotism. Individuals with this personality exaggerate their accomplishments and talents, have a sense of entitlement, lack empathy or concern for others, are preoccupied with envy and jealousy, and have an arrogant attitude.

I've heard it said that narcissists don't suffer from their mental illness—the rest of us do. The narcissist has no image of self: their image is defined by the people around them, usually family. How good or bad they view themselves depends on how they manage and control these people in their life. Narcissists are arrogant, manipulative, have a sense of entitlement, and demand obedience and loyalty from their family members and friends. It can be truly horrible to be in relationships with them. The narcissist is absorbed by fantasies of unlimited success, and seeks constant attention. They also feel like they are immune to the consequences of their actions, and usually blame others for it. The narcissist is like the famous movie star Joan Crawford in "Mommy Dearest": everything revolved around her moods, and God help anyone that was in the way when she went on her rampages.

I have a lot of experience dealing with narcissists. The minute they enter a room, and you hear their footsteps, you have to brace yourself for a tongue lashing if they are in a bad mood. You are constantly walking on eggshells around their bad tempers. My dad was an ex-marine who was in command in all of us. He was also a classic narcissist, like the character in "The Great Santini". He constantly criticized all of us when we were home, but was very concerned about "what people will think" when he was out in public. He always made sure that we always gave off the impression of "the perfect family". He wasn't concerned about what people thought about us, he was more nervous about what people thought about HIM. He was so into what others thought about him that he thought that my mother's funeral was a great opportunity for him to "work the room". He behaved as if everyone came to see him, rather than pay last respects to his wife. When the event was over, he wanted us to take our mom's urn because he "didn't deal well with death", and we refused. He begrudgingly put the urn into his trunk next to his golf clubs, where it remained for a year. Whether he was in denial of the fact that he'd lost his wife, and just didn't know how to show his feelings, we'll never know. Usually, the narcissist rarely shows their feelings in private, only when there is audience so that they can put on a show.

Here is a story about a narcissistic mother who constantly belittled her daughter (key word here, *belittled*), always telling her how she was not good enough, thin enough, or pretty enough. She even went as far as to always try on her daughter's clothes stating that "they look much better on me than you", even though she was 26 years older than her and not nearly as pretty. This verbal chastising, as well as physical cruelty (hitting with a belt to make a point), went on until one day the daughter snapped and could no longer tolerate the verbal and physical abuse. She took scissors to her mother's face and told her "If you ever lay a hand on me again, or torment me, I will kill you!" The mother couldn't believe what was happening, and screamed "Stop--you don't know what you're doing--don't hurt me—you're crazy!" The daughter lifted the scissors as if she were going to stab her, and then threw the scissors in the opposite direction. No, she was not crazy or going to kill her: she had just had enough. The mother never laid a hand on the daughter again. In the daughter's case, the mother would take and take and take until the daughter had to lay down boundaries, which were never crossed again. The moral of this story is that when dealing with a narcissist, you must establish boundaries: these people are basically cowards that overcompensate their inadequacies by bullying, and you have to let them know when they've pushed you too far.

We've summarized Category B personality disorders, which most us fall into, one way or the other. As far as the other categories, you're too busy with the straitjacket, meds and rubber room to worry about your family trust. Luckily for you, you're probably chemically sedated and don't have to worry about these depressing things.

If your parent has any of the above personality disorders AND Alzheimer's, don't bother even getting out of bed in the morning—your life is going to be living hell. The above behaviors will be even MORE exaggerated and intensified until you won't even recognize who your parents are. Alzheimer's and dementia can create monstrous behavior in even the nicest of people. My friend Victor's father was a kind man who worked at the Catholic church helping people. Alzheimer's crept in, and he became paranoid, abusive, and had to be taken away one day kicking and screaming in a strait jacket. As Betty Davis once said "Getting old ain't for sissies!".

Chapter Four

Vultures In Pinstriped Suits

If you have a lawyer written into your family trust, a word of advice: buy a spy pen or spyglasses and record any meeting that you attend with them so that you can review it later. This espionage equipment can be purchased on the internet. I bought the spy pen and it works remarkably well: it can videotape and record sound up to one hour. I wish that someone had told me this when my whole nightmare began. I don't think things would have gone as far as they did. Yes, it could be construed as illegal to videotape someone without them knowing it, but after all, you might be dealing with a crook anyway, and you will need to review what just happened to you for $350 an hour. Here's what I think you really should be getting for your money with a trust attorney:

1/ When an attorney holds money for a client, they must place it into an interest-bearing trust account, the interest belonging to the client.

2/ The client's trust account must include money received on the client's behalf, and advances for costs, expenses and fees.

3/The attorney must notify their clients of money received on their behalf and promptly pay money that is due.

4/The attorney must act in their client's best interest. They are not permitted to use their client's trust accounts without their permission.

All of this seems like common sense, you probably think. Also, when you're paying top dollar for this service, you're under the impression that the attorneys, having passed the bar and being licensed in the state that you are in, are held to very high standards, and wouldn't DARE break any of these rules. Guess what? THEY DO. On a regular basis.

Robert M. Telthorst, a trust attorney, was indicted for fraud after an investigation by the FBI. From November 2005 to August 2011 he executed what was in essence a "Ponzi" scheme in which he took money from his clients and used it to benefit himself and to cover up the fact that he was taking money from his other clients' trust accounts. He diverted funds from a charitable trust to a dummy investment that went directly to him, turning $80,000 into $1750, and also magically turned a $463,344 trust account for two children into a bank balance of $150! He is serving time for this, of course, but think about it: how many of these attorneys are out there doing this WITHOUT GETTING CAUGHT?

Like most people, I walked into my father's attorney's office with the assumption that my dad had hired a good attorney who was going to protect the trust and his assets. I didn't really think about it at the time, but the office was in an expensive skyscraper on the 12th floor, overlooking the city. A fleeting thought went past me about how much it must cost, but I soon dismissed it when I was greeted warmly by Dick, the oh so kind Christian attorney. We all sat down at the big conference table.

You know that you have a problem when your father's attorney calls you "the kids" when he's the same age as you. This condescending attitude was done intentionally to demean our positions, especially when our father was present. RED FLAG. Dick, the oh so kind lawyer, had it all figured out: he was the king of meetings. Phone, office, conferences....but he NEVER PUT ANYTHING IN WRITING. RED FLAG #2. Word to the wise: any attorney who refuses to put what they say into writing usually has something to hide. This was the start of endless meetings that cost $350 to $450 an hour, and nothing was ever accomplished or settled, except for the fact that the attorney was racking up a huge bill to charge the trust. Needless to say, we did a year of endless meetings that went nowhere.

At first I thought Dick was an okay guy, just trying to make things work. He certainly acted sincere. KEY WORD: ACTED. RED FLAG #3: Never let your guard down with a lawyer, especially one who has written himself into your family TRUST. There were many telltale signs, but I just didn't see them. Or truth be told, the whole situation was so convoluted and depressing that I just didn't want to deal with it. As my dad's mental capacity diminished, I thought it was a good idea to have him retire from the Trust, and let my brother, Dick, and myself take over, as we were listed on the Trust as successor trustees. At least that way I could have a say and some sort of financial control over my brother and the lawyer, who were draining the Trust at $5,000 a month EACH.

Dick, the oh so kind Christian lawyer drew up the "Resignation as Trustee" paper for my Dad after 10 meetings. Mind you, it took 10 meetings of basically showing up for nothing to get to this point. The papers were drawn, and notarized, and my father signed with no objections. I thought to myself "Finally we were getting somewhere. Now I can put a stop to these endless expensive meetings and legal fees, not to mention all of the money I lost from taking time off work to come to them". VICTORY AT LAST!

So, Dick has my brother and I believing that we were now trustees, making decisions. Basically he was letting us believe we were trustees so that he could continue to charge the Trust ridiculous fees, thinking that no one would question him. After all, my dad had led Dick, the oh so kind Christian lawyer to believe that both of his kids were complete losers. Only half-right, Dick.

I started requesting itemized statements, since all of my dad's bills were now being paid by Dick's office. It seemed that not only did Dick have all of my dad's stocks, bonds, 401k plan, et cetera, he now did the bills and virtually everything that involved my dad's money. RED FLAG #5: Never ever let one person have control over EVERYTHING, especially a lawyer.

I started requesting to see all of the invoices. After all, I was a TRUSTEE, RIGHT? WRONG AGAIN. I questioned one of the bills where "WE'RE FRIENDS" Dick charged the Trust $5,000 for one month of his services. Here's the email that I received from him:

> From: Dick Richards. Esq.
> To: Katherine Steel
>
> You are not a trustee yet. Your father has not given permission to activate the document. He is still the trustee.
>
> Best, Dick

I thought to myself "Am I on DRUGS? What about the office visit, the signing of papers, the notary? Somebody PLEASE FILL ME IN, I'M LOST, THIS DOES NOT COMPUTE!". I questioned Dick in yet another phone meeting, saying "But I am a trustee. We filled out and notarized the papers!" He informed me in his very kind Christian manner that the papers were there when my dad was ready to step down. Ready? My dad's estate was bleeding money to him and my brother. If that's not ready, when is? My dad, when he was in his right mind, was really CHEAP. If he comprehended how much money was flying out the window, he would have been FURIOUS.

I SAID TO MYSELF: "WE'RE IN BIG TROUBLE NOW".

Dick, the oh so kind lawyer had now proclaimed himself "Emperor" of our family Trust. He was now acting as EXECUTOR, TRUSTEE and MEDICAL EXAMINER, as he alone had the power to decide when my father should "resign". My father, at this time, remember, couldn't balance a checkbook, couldn't pass his driver's test, couldn't make change, and couldn't carry on a phone conversation without forgetting words. In other words, his brain was floating somewhere out in the cosmos, and wasn't coming back.

So I had had enough. I decided at that point that I would consult another lawyer about the situation. I called a lawyer that I had dealt with in previous years for contracts. He had a department that could handle trusts. He turned me over to a sharp lady named Stephanie. We discussed the case, and I gave her the endless e-mails that I had kept, which were incriminating to my brother and the lawyer. NOTE TO THE WISE:

Keep all correspondence, especially emails. You WILL NEED THEM, BELIEVE ME, as they can be used as LEVERAGE. Stephanie read our Trust, and then read all of my carbon copied emails from my brother and the attorney. She was especially interested in the following one. The "silver bullet", so to speak:

> To: Dick Richards, Esq.
> Subject: Dad's spending
>
> Dad told me yesterday that he went to the Wells Fargo and opened up a checking account. They are going to also be sending him checks. As you know, my dad needs help in every way possible when he attempts a

financial transaction. I think it's okay to expect him to have some cash on him, but I don't want to see him taken advantage of (*except by him*!). I guess the question is; how risky is this to his account?

Robbie Jr.

Dick responded with this email:

To: Robbie Jr.

Check in on your father periodically. When the checks arrive, take them home with you. Let me know when you receive them.

Thanks, Dick

Okay. My dad is the trustee, and the attorney is instructing my brother to take away his checkbook, knowing that he should not have them in his possession because he is not of sound mind. Stephanie could not believe that Dick would put this in writing, but he did. Most trusts, including ours, instruct the trustee to RETIRE if they are not of sound mind. Stephanie recommended that we write a letter to Dick, and instruct him to honor the trust and allow my father to resign. Here's an excerpt from it:

From: Stephanie Meyer, Esq.

Re: Steel Trust

Dear Mr. Richards,

I am writing this letter on behalf of my client, Katherine Steel, in regards to the Steel Revocable Trust. Last

July, Robert Steel was diagnosed with dementia. During a meeting in your office with my client and Mr. Steel, he signed a letter of resignation as sole Trustee. If that is the case, then Mr. Steel had the legal capacity to execute the legal document, and Katherine and Robbie Steel, and yourself are now co-trustees.

You recently informed my client that you have not been instructed to "activate" his resignation, and therefore neither Katherine or Robbie are Trustees. You have not provided Katherine with a copy of the document, so she has no way to independently determine who, if anyone, is currently the Trustee.

You have refused Katherine access to these documents, and she has no way to see trust financial transactions since last July. I am sure that you are aware that misappropriation of assets by persons hired by the elderly is far from rare. Your refusal to give Katherine the document leaves her to conclude that something is wrong, and she has no way to investigate the matter short of court action unless we can resolve this situation.

Since you have not "activated" the resignation of Robert Steel, then Mr. Steel is still the Trustee. Since Mr. Steel has been diagnosed with dementia, and you are now administering the Steel Revocable Trust without being the Trustee and without any oversight, the situation is ripe for abuse, which is why my client, Katherine Steel, seeks a change in the situation and a full accounting and audit of any transactions that your firm has made since this situation arose. She is also very concerned that her brother, Robbie Steel, has received over $300,000 in trust assets over the years.

Please provide my office with a copy of the document that was executed in your office last August which Katherine believes to be a Trustee resignation signed by her father, Robert Steel. Please also provide my office with a copy of the latest amendment to the Trust, power of attorney, and Financial directive pertaining to who is actually administering the Trust and how it is being administered. After reviewing these documents, we will be in a better position to confer with you. Please do not hesitate to contact me about this matter.

Sincerely,

Stephanie Meyer, Esq.

Stephanie sent the letter to Dick, thinking we would get an immediate response and open up a dialogue.

WRONG. Dick panicked, and went out and hired his own lawyer at the EXPENSE OF MY FATHER'S TRUST, to represent him. This was totally out of left field, not what Stephanie or I expected. Stephanie got a call from Dick's attorney and he told her that we could all have a meeting if we all agreed in writing to never use the email that Dick wrote instructing my brother to take the checkbook away. Stephanie told him absolutely not. THEY FREAKED OUT. Stephanie told me that she had never seen grown men act like such children before. Unfortunately, now the $250 letter I paid Stephanie to write turned into a $900 dollar retainer. Not liking this idea at all, but not knowing what else to do, I signed the retainer, figuring I'd only go up to $900 at the most. After all, Dick, the oh so kind lawyer went to church with my dad--he couldn't be that crooked, could he?

WRONG AGAIN. If you really think about it, a church is a great place to go for new clients, especially if it's a lot of elderly rich people trying to make a place for themselves in the hereafter. Never think that a lawyer who finds clients in a church is good only because he attends church with you—it's quite possible that he is there to harvest the life savings of people like your parents.

So after going through $900 in just about two seconds to find out that I had a case, and that yes, Dick the Lawyer had acted in an unethical manner, and yes, my brother had also violated the trust by taking large amounts of money, I was left with the decision to go on with Stephanie and pursue legal action, which started to get expensive: the $900 retainer quickly climbed to $3000 in the blink of an eye after a volley of letters back and forth from Stephanie and Dick's attorney (the one the Trust was paying for!). To save money on court costs, I thought that maybe we could negotiate with Dick, but they wanted us to take the e-mails off the table. Hell no, we wouldn't take the e-mails off the table: they were the only real evidence we had.

Even if you like your lawyer, you will quickly become acquainted with the attorney's TIMEKEEPER SUMMARY. Every month they send you their bill, and it bills you for the hours that they have spent on your case. They can bill you for phone calls, emails, Xerox copies, and even if they are thinking about you while they are sitting on the toilet. When you open up these timekeeper summaries, you find out just how high your blood pressure can go. I suggest sitting down when you read these things, taking it all in, then going out and screaming at the top of your lungs. I was especially pissed when I read "$100 for phone call" on the summary. It was a phone call that I had made JUST TO MAKE AN APPOINTMENT!

To make a long story short, $3000 later and nowhere closer to saving the "Bank of Bob" from my brother and Dick, I lost my job and had to let Stephanie go. The case was good…I just did not have the dough. I figured I needed $25,000 to a $50,000 to win the case. I just didn't have it.

When you're dealing with financial advisors and lawyers, it takes a long time to realize that you are being had. By the time you realize what they've done, all of your money might be gone. My advice for dealing with financial advisors is to ONLY USE THEM FOR A CONSULTATION. Really think twice if you are going to hand your finances over to them. If you are stuck with them, make sure that you check and recheck every single transaction. No one watches or takes care of your money better than YOU. You could end up like the people in the following story, who had the misfortune of hiring Stacy Sheedy as their financial advisor.

A lawyer and financial advisor, Stacy Sheedy represented elderly clients in her firm and had the responsibility of investing and watching out for their assets. The clients were in deep s**t with her as their financial advisor. The investigation began after one client reported thefts from an account that supported their grandmother with Alzheimer's who lived in a nursing home. Sheedy, who took responsibility for the guardianship account, made at least 32 unauthorized withdrawals totaling $172,000. Investigators proceeded to audit her other accounts. They examined Sheedy's role in another family trust, for which she had served as trustee. A brokerage account within the trust started at $501,000 when Sheedy became trustee, and was drained to only $168 over a period of a few years.

When family members asked why they were no longer receiving brokerage statements from the account, Sheedy told them that she had invested the funds in a bond fund and periodically sent them statements from the Indiana Small Cap Bond fund. Guess what? NO FUNDS EVER EXISTED! Again, check your bank statements and paperwork, and make sure whatever you have purchased IS REAL. Sheedy made unauthorized withdrawals of $412,500 from the trust account this way. Each family's trust was cleaned out by her. Sheedy became greedy, to say the least. Each trust was a lifetime of hard earned money that no family member will ever see. Sheedy's new residence is the Indianapolis state penitentiary. She'll be residing with them for the next eight years. Maybe she'll give some of the convicts investment advice. If she screws them over, at least THEY'LL KNOW HOW TO DEAL WITH HER!

There's an old saying: "Sometimes it's easier to rob you with a fountain pen than it is with a gun."

That was certainly the case of two young men who were supposed to inherit money from a trust when they turned eighteen. The sole trustee, Robert Buschmohle, had embezzled $389,000 out of a living trust created for the benefit of the two boys.

When the young men neared the disbursement age, their mother called Buschmohle to find out when they would receive their payments. Buschmohle failed to return her calls, so in frustration she complained to the Attorney Grievance Commission, which contacted the police. The commission has the authority to investigate and file charges against an attorney for potential professional wrongdoing to the Attorney Discipline Board.

"This family placed their trust in this man, and he stole everything down to their last penny," a spokesman for the family said. Buschmohle wrote checks to himself over a four year period, eventually "draining the trust account in its entirety." Buschmohle is facing twenty years in prison. As for the boys, NA DA. ZERO. ZIP. Why? Because no one was paying attention to the man behind the curtain. This happens ALL THE TIME. Everyone is aware of the famous cases like Anna Nicole Smith, and Leona Helmsley, but financial advisors and attorneys are stealing and embezzling regular trusting client's money EVERY DAY. After all, the money's in a TRUST. RIGHT? WRONG.

Chapter Five

Do It Yourself Law If You Can Take It

All of this stuff hit me in 2009, and the recession had also hit my career hard. Finding myself unemployed, and without the money to continue with the lawyer, I was forced to seek alternative methods to keep forging on. I do not recommend this journey for the faint of heart. It is a nightmare of bureaucrats and pencil pushers where no one wants to do anything, and the answer is always "NO". That said, I decided to stop with the attorneys and take the matter into my own hands.

Like an idiot, I tried to reason with my father. I showed him all of the incriminating evidence, including the letter from the attorney telling my brother to take his checkbook away. I found out the hard way that this information just could not find it's way into his head. This is when I found out that

DEMENTIA IS CONTAGIOUS! I'd ask him five minutes later to repeat what I had said, and of course, he couldn't. I actually started to get as distracted as he was. Dementia has it's own conversation level—it's either pleasantly stupid, or there is no conversation at all. Difficult things cannot be discussed, I found out. At times I was so frustrated with him that I started yelling at him to understand, but I still got the same blank "this isn't pleasant" stare. Maybe it's the Kool-Aid they were giving him in the rest home, who knows?

That's when I decided to try the "The Social Worker Family Mending Option". Armed with my incriminating emails and nasty letter to Dick, the oh so kind lawyer, I decided to appeal to the social workers at the home my father was in. I'm thinking "Social Worker—usually a kind, wonderful person who cares about others—*they'll* understand." Unfortunately, my TV version social worker concept wasn't what I got. I found out that they didn't like me, as Dick, the oh so kind attorney had told my father that the reason I had hired a lawyer was because I was only after his money. I decided to go and meet with them. Surely I could work this false concept out! My visit to the home was not good. Big distrust. Bad vibes everywhere. They knew my brother better than I, and of course, that made sense. He had to collect checks weekly from my dad, so he was always there! I asked if the social worker could set up a family meeting, so I could try and reason with both my father and brother about what was going on with the attorney. My brother wouldn't do it. With that, the social worker bowed out. There was nothing she could do. I decided to go to the top of the place, and talk to the director of social services there. More denial, more sidestepping the issue, more f**k you, basically.

There's always the Internet!

I didn't have much of a family any longer, but I still had my emails. I started to scour the internet for solutions. The word "Elder Abuse" kept coming up next to the "Rascal" ads. I found an "Elder Abuse Task Force", and emailed the contact person. To my surprise, she emailed back and referred me to "Adult Protective Services". The investigator, a nice Russian lady, wanted to see everything. I gave her my emails, the Trust, attorney letters, anything I could get my hands on. Then...she vanished. She didn't return my calls, emails, anything. That's when I tried

The "Phone call to the Superior"

Always go to the top. I hadn't heard from the Russian lady for a month. She vanished. Maybe the KGB got her. I didn't know. I did the famous "Phone Call to the Superior"—I should never have waited even that long. Lesson #3900: never wait more than a few days before going to the top for an answer. The superior, of course, didn't call me back, but suddenly, out of the blue, the Russian lady returned from Siberia full of information. She had met with the social workers at the home, and with my father on several occasions, and finally was successful in getting a psychiatrist to examine my father. His diagnosis? Dementia! But at least Adult Protective Services knew. The nice Russian lady had to go on maternity leave, so she referred my case to a really nice man, Adolfo, who was the head of her department. He assured me that my problems were over, as there was enough incriminating evidence to move the case forward—hallelujah! He was referring the case to probate court to proceed with a third party conservatorship.

That fleeting "Winning" feeling

Yes! I'm a winner after losing for so long. Where's the prize? Door number 3....and it says NOT! As they say in Monopoly, "Do Not Pass Go"! Probate court kicked the case out on a technicality. I was in shock. How could that be? I was now in the hands of Mr. Loo, from probate, who officiously told me "You must file a claim yourself. File with Alameda county...or try for conservatorship yourself!" He then gave me the address of a free clinic, and told me that I can do it myself for FREE. Believe me, FREE IS SO NOT FREE.

Can't afford a lawyer? Welcome to the County.

Sounds bad? It is. I've lived in San Francisco my whole life, but never had the opportunity to visit the county courthouse. After you've been searched up and down and have proceeded through the metal detectors, you find yourself walking down long, tattered aisles graced by the forlorn looks of sad people from all cultures, and all walks of life. I watched as all of the attorneys in their cheap suits and lousy footwear struggled with their rolly wheel suitcases. One poor attorney looked like she was not only struggling with her rolly wheel, she was struggling to stay inside her corporate nun suit which was a couple sizes too small. I sat next to a frustrated guy in a leather jacket who commented as a sad security guard walked by "That man looks like he really enjoys his job!" He then turned to me and said "Can you imagine coming to work at this place every day?" I agreed. It was miserable. After waiting for a long period of time, you realize that you are involved in a miserable journey in a building that equals the worst of Russian "proletariat" architecture. You almost expect a foul looking woman with black shoes, a babushka and a regulation mole on the side of her face to walk by. You have to be bilingual to work at a place like this. There were whole Mexican families walking around in a daze as if they were visiting Mars for the first time. After waiting for the Hernandez family to finally understand what the bilingual attorney was saying to them, I got to talk to an attorney that looked as if he was on the last leg of his career. His eyes told me that he could give a crap about absolutely nothing, and that years of dealing with the problems of dysfunctional families had left him completely emotionless and desperately awaiting his coffee break. After three attempts of blowing me off to another department, he finally acquiesced, and allowed me to plead my own tragic case to him. He gave me just enough information to ask for more, and sent me off to another room, where a bright-eyed young attorney wanted to help me, but realized that she was out of her league. She discussed some options with me, handed me a worthless printed sheet of lawyer referrals and sent me back out to the struggling masses.

The guy in the leather jacket saw me and asked "Did you get what you needed?" "Worth about as much as I paid—nothing" I answered him back. "They are only interested in you if you are penniless" he told me. I wished him good luck. He'd need it.

Free is not free, as I said before. Turns out that conservatorship is costly. Court filing fees, process server fees, dragging your family into a whole ugly messy court trial, and then you get the bill. WHAT A BARGAIN. Thanks Mr. Loo. I even went to back to my expensive attorney just to make sure I wouldn't be disinherited by filing for conservatorship. What a mistake that was. I got another bill from him charging me for the phone call I made to make the appointment! Then I called them to challenge it, and he charged me for that! Help! What a financial cesspool!

"Phone call to the Superior" revisited.

Since Mr. Loo now wouldn't return my phone calls, and I was getting bills from lawyers that were from outer space, I felt like I had just capsized my boat and was sinking fast. MAYDAY, MAYDAY. What next? How could I have forgotten the most important thing? THE PHONE CALL TO THE SUPERIOR! I got the name of the director of mental health from the internet, got his answering machine, and left my saga on it. Weird thing---after that, MR. LOO SUDDENLY CALLED. What a coincidence! Mr. Loo was not happy. Mr. Loo was irritated, but accommodating, and sent me a packet to fill out. ANOTHER DAY bit the dust. As hard as it is, keep a record of all time you've put into this miserable process. People, names, phone numbers, et cetera. You'd think that you could just pull up the old letter that started the investigation, but no. YOU MUST SUFFER. And suffer you shall as you re-experience the whole miserable mess as you rewrite it yet another time. After that, you put it into the fax machine, pull the trigger, then WAIT and HOPE that it will fall into the right hands and actually go somewhere.

After filling Adolfo from Adult Protective Services in on my saga, he told me to file my own complaint with probate, claiming "undue influence". Lucky me, I got "Richard", quite possibly the laziest state worker I have ever encountered. He made a DMV worker look ambitious. It made me think of the joke:

What do you get when you cross a state worker with a donkey? *A lazy ass!*

Anyway, Richard was MIA for weeks. First, not in the office. Next, in training. Next...had a cold. After weeks of phone tag to his superior, I finally got to talk to the infamous Richard. I spent an hour on the phone explaining my situation to him, and relating to my file which he had never received. I found myself telling my saga once again, to another county worker. Ah, the never ending saga. Beyond FRUSTRATION. If I had only been paid for all of the hours I'd put into this quagmire. Now I found out that the most important part of my case was missing from Richard's investigation: THE FINDINGS from the DOCTOR about my dad's incompetence. I asked him about the psych test. He asked me WHAT TEST? I thought to myself, how could we have talked to each other before without him knowing about this? How could this guy have even started an investigation of any kind without knowing about it? That sinking feeling came back again. Like one of those nightmares where you're screaming for help and nothing is coming out! Help! How does anyone get anything done this way? Your case is lost in paperwork shuffled from one side of the desk to another. Maybe if you're lucky, your case will fall on the desk next to the donut and the cup of coffee, and while they're wiping the food stains off, they'll read your file. The worst of it is the feeling of one step forward, and ten steps back. I then knew what a phone solicitor felt like. Here's a sample of what a conversation with a state worker is like:

> Me: "Hi, I'm Katherine, let me tell you a story about my demented father. It all started back when....."
>
> State Worker: "Uh huh." (he checks his email, then goes on Facebook) "Uh huh".
>
> Me: "…and then I took it to Adult Protective Services, and…"
>
> State Worker: "Right". (He checks out the pop up ad for flatter abs) "Interesting".
>
> Me: "APS finally got a test done in November that confirmed the dementia."
>
> State Worker: "Well, we can't really do much without a dementia diagnosis."
>
> Me: "You mean you don't have it?"
>
> State Worker: "No. Has one ever been done?"
>
> Me: "I just told you one was done in November?"
>
> State Worker: "Oh. You'd better send it over, then!"
>
> Me: "How can I send it to you when the state is the one that did the test?"

State Worker: "I'll look into it."

After hanging up, I took time to enter just how much more time I'd wasted into my own timekeeper. I must've been into thousands of wasted hours at that point. After reviewing my timekeeper I again had my recurring sinking feeling. IT WAS THE SLOW ROAD TO HELL.......that's right, I'd been at this for two years now.

The doubts began to creep in again. I could have waited for Richard the State Worker to do something, but it probably wouldn't happen until I was in a retirement home with Alzheimer's myself. Time for action! Time to kick ass! Screw it, I went to the D.A.!

Below is a copy of the letter I wrote to the district attorney:

Dear _____,

I believe that this case should be investigated by the elder abuse task force for violation of California civil code 1575 "undue influence".

My father, Robert Steel, has been diagnosed with dementia by two doctors. The first was Dr. James Cordmeyer on September 15, 2008, and the second diagnosis was done by a doctor hired by Adult Protective Services in November 2009 and done at the Sunny Acres Retirement Home, where my father resides. Per my conversation with Adolfo Ramirez of Adult Protective Services, the Doctor's findings were that my father is financially incompetent and needs a conservator to look after his finances.

I contacted Adult Protective Services in July 2008 because of an email I was carbon copied. The email was from Dick Richards, my father's trust attorney, to my brother, Robbie Steel Jr., instructing him to take my father's checkbook away from him. (see attached). I suspected that financial elder abuse had been committed by them. Since Dr. Cordmeyer's dementia diagnosis, large amounts of money have been used from the Trust to clear up my brother's credit card debts, to buy him a car, and pay his mortgage payments. Mr. Richards, who is not only the drafting attorney of the Trust, is also my father's financial planner, and has himself listed as Successor Trustee along with my brother and I. Every financial transaction of my father goes through Mr. Richard's office, Acme Financial Consultants, and the last bill I saw from them was $5,000 for a month's work. I believe that Mr. Richards has been acting illegally as both Trustee and Conservator since Dr. Cordmeyer's diagnosis. He also refuses transparency of all of his financial transactions in my father's behalf, and is ignoring the Trust instructions for my father to retire as Trustee when he is found financially incompetent. My fear is at the rate that Mr. Richards and my brother, Robbie Steel Jr., are liquidating my father's assets, they will soon, if they have not already, sell whatever assets that are remaining. I think that they should both be investigated by your office for possible criminal activity.

Sincerely,

Katherine Steel

Surprise! I got a phone call from the district attorney himself. I was impressed. I again explained my case. He told me that he would take me on if probate decided it was a good enough case to prosecute. This left me optimistic! Justice! Light at the end of the tunnel! I finally talked to Richard, the lazy ass probate investigator, and he informed me that he was seeking a form from the psychiatrist that did an evaluation on my dad. If he received that, then he would go to the courts and ask the judge for a conservator for our trust. But, there was a catch! He had to interview my brother and the lawyer. I knew that my brother would never talk to probate, because he referred everything to Dick, the charming insincere lawyer, who referred it to HIS lawyer. Dick would then pay his attorney fees via our Trust under the premise that I was attacking it. My big hope was that this case would be taken to the courts, where at least my brother and Dick would have some explaining to do.

Two weeks went by, and I tried to make contact at least once a week to the probate office, to let them know I was not giving up, and that I was still alive and wanted to see what pathetic progress had been made. If things ran any slower they would rot.

JUDGEMENT: DENIED!

Richard, the lazy ass probate investigator, finally got back to me. He probably called me during his donut break and was fitting me in between bites. After five months and hundreds of hours of work on my part, I was told in a split second, "I'm sorry--there isn't enough evidence to go to court and ask for a third party conservator. Even though the state doctor declared your father incompetent in his written evaluation, he refused to fill out the formal declaration of incompetence, as he did not want to be involved in a court case." *Another* lazy state worker—the state psychiatrist.

Richard also informed me that they were so bogged down with abuse cases that he was only handling the cases where the victims were being locked in closets or drooling and crawling on the floor. He then concluded that since my family had money that I should hire an attorney and handle it on my own. A COMPLETE BRUSHOFF.

I was dumbfounded. For the last 5 months I had been going on the assumption that the doctor had already stated that my father was financially incompetent, but I was never allowed access to view the actual papers. My only reference was the phone conversations that I had had with Adolfo of Adult Protective Services.

As a last ditch effort, I went back to Adolfo and asked him "WHAT JUST HAPPENED?" If indeed there was nothing in writing that recommended a conservatorship, then it looked like the FAT LADY HAD SUNG. And, if that indeed was the truth, then I had no option but to walk away from the whole stinking mess. JUST WALK AWAY, how sad. So much work, time, and 2 years of my life, and for what? This by no means changed the truth that my brother and the lawyer were wrong for what they were doing, but in this country, if you don't have a dime, don't waste your time. This a country where you can kill your wife and get off if you have enough money. I just didn't have the bucks to fight the lawyer and my brother, especially since the Trust would pay for any of their legal bills.

Even though I decided to let this process go, I could have still gone forward to seek a conservatorship. It would have at least put my brother and the lawyer in check, as they would have had to justify all of the missing funds to a judge. Again, I would have had to have shelled out money for court costs, paper filings, etc., and would have had to have represented myself against their hired attorney PAID FOR BY THE TRUST! Basically, it would have been like eating myself alive. I decided to abort the process, regroup and rethink my strategy.

Chapter Six

Testamentary Capacity

This term describes the state of mind of a person when they are signing a legal document, and can be the keystone of the legitimacy of trusts and wills. Were they aware of what they were signing? Did they really choose Little Jimmy over Crabby Cathy to be executor, or did Little Jimmy influence them to sign in his favor?

This is a very slippery slope. According to the law, a demented person can legally have one brief moment of lucidity, sign a document, and then go back to whatever planet in the cosmos they think that they are on. The interpretation of "testamentary capacity" in courtrooms can mean victory or defeat to an heir, and if undue influence is detected, prison time. Endless hours of courtroom time, and millions of billable hours of attorney time are spent debating this interpretation every day. So, if you believe that a family member, unscrupulous attorney, or someone else has used undue influence on your parents to change a will in their favor, the phrase "testamentary capacity" will undoubtedly be your battleground. The way the phrase is interpreted is so vague that you could have all of the evidence in the world and the decision could go against you.

When you've been unjustly screwed out of your inheritance, you have several choices. You can walk away from the whole thing, buy yourself a bottle of Jack Daniels, do the lost weekend thing and give up, or you can hire an attorney and fight for what is yours. Envision yourself in a movie with Spencer Tracy as your attorney and kick some ass!

In my case, my attorney requested documents from Dick, the oh so kind attorney, to no avail. He refused to give them to us. The only way we could have persuaded Dick to give them to us is through the process of discovery, which would only occur if we had sued him for malpractice and financial elder abuse. In other words, put up or shut up. Pay an attorney a retainer, and start reaching into your pockets for court costs. Don't kid yourself, it is a tough journey. Do yourself a favor and watch Charles Dicken's "Bleak House" on Masterpiece Theater before you start. It's a story about an heir that is told he is to inherit a fortune from an estate, but the will is so convoluted and messed up that when the money is finally disbursed, the ATTORNEYS TAKE IT ALL, leaving the poor bastard penniless. It's the way any lawsuit can go...you can end up with nothing, and the lawyers and courts take it all. The LAWYERS ALWAYS WIN. You can win, too, if you limit how much THEY GET.

What you really want to have happen is to have ammunition for your case, and scare the living crap out of the other party's attorney, so that you can settle out of court. You need a "smoking gun" document—something that undoubtedly proves your case. It needs to be an undisputed "caught in the act" document, or a signed, notarized contract that supports your position.

I thought I had a "smoking gun" with my father's autopsy. Analysis of brain tissue showed that he was in the advanced stages of Alzheimer's when he died, and had been so for years. I took the autopsy to my attorney and thought he'd jump at the chance to file the lawsuit. NOT. Why not? "testamentary capacity"! As bad off as my dad was, it could be debated in court that for one split second of time he was lucid enough to make financial decisions. There have been cases of people having their parents change their wills on their deathbed, and actually holding their hands to sign their names to the document. It's actually legal to "assist" a person signing a document this way. If that doesn't smack of undue influence, I don't know what does. Anything can happen in a courtroom, however, and you could win, depending on how well you've kept records. KEEP EVERYTHING. And I mean EVERYTHING: all correspondence, emails, and any letters that your parents may have written could make the difference between receiving nothing and receiving everything. The weird thing about law is that the most innocuous of documents could become the "Rosetta Stone" of your case. It could be a handwritten letter from your father to your sibling that states that money that was given was a "loan". It could be the way your sibling, or other inheritance crook, left clues to their crime. If you can get access to these files, and your attorney smells smoke, you may have a case.

When I say show your files to an attorney, I MEAN AN ATTORNEY THAT YOU CAN TRUST. Find an attorney by asking friends of yours for references. Check them out by going on your state bar website and see if there are any complaints about them. If they are counseling you to do something that doesn't feel right, ASK ANOTHER ATTORNEY. It's a pain, but it is imperative that you find the right person for your case. The wrong one could cost you EVERYTHING. If you search the internet, you will find cases where unscrupulous attorneys actually work in tandem with caretakers to write wills and trusts for the elderly that give them the power to liquidate their assets before the family even knows what happened to them. In my case, Dick, the oh so kind attorney, wrote himself into my dad's trust as a TRUSTEE. This is a BIG RED FLAG IN CALIFORNIA. California law is suspicious of any attorney that does this, and if they write themselves in as a beneficiary, it's more than a red flag: it's a big, STINKING RED FLAG!

It's rare, but a testamentary capacity case can be won. Two different sets of kids from the two wives of a stepfather who was dying from cancer got into a fight when a "deathbed will" that favored one set over the other was presented in court to challenge a will that was written years before. The kids who were to be screwed by the "deathbed will" claimed that the other kids had exercised "undue influence" on the father during his last dying days, having him sign it while he lacked "testamentary capacity". The kids who had him sign the "deathbed will" claimed that he had changed his mind about the distribution of assets because they took care of him during his last days.

The case got so bad that it turned into a six day jury trial. High stakes indeed, and big $$$$ to the attorneys. The attorney for the potentially screwed kids presented evidence that in the weeks prior to, and after his execution of the "deathbed will", the father was taking prescribed narcotic drugs, which had side effects of hallucinations, disorientation, and impaired mental and physical performance. He was also taking an antidepressant that could cause confusion, impaired mental concentration, and hallucinations, and had increased levels of narcotics in his body due to his liver not functioning because of his cancer. A pharmacology expert testified that with that much pain medication, and a damaged liver, the father would not be rationally sane. A hospice worker testified that the father had difficulty completing his sentences, was forgetful, and even denied having siblings, despite the fact that his sister was in the room with him most of the time. Their attorney also presented testimony that the terms of the "deathbed will" were inconsistent with their father's repeated statements to others that he wished to treat all of his children equally.

In the end, the jurors believed that indeed the will was signed under undue influence, and voted that the "deathbed will" was invalid. The other kids appealed it all the way to the Supreme Court of Georgia. According to this court, and under the statutes of that state, "a will is not valid if anything destroys the testator's freedom of volition, such as undue influence whereby the will of another is substituted for the wishes of the testator." Based on a review of the evidence, the court determined that there was sufficient support to uphold the jury's verdict. So much for getting signatures "under the gun": the kids who had obtained the "deathbed will" not only had to pay the legal and court costs for the original suit, they had to pay for the State Supreme Court costs as well, completely wiping out their inheritance.

The problem with basing your case on "testamentary capacity" is that it is a 50/50 success rate—it all depends on the judge or jury. A woman who always smelled gas and thought that her husband was poisoning her, even though he wasn't, decided to leave him nothing in her last minute will. He challenged it, but the courts upheld her will because during her paranoid delusions, she did have rational moments of lucidity. "Moments of lucidity" is the crux of the testamentary capacity argument.

In the case of Ouderkirk vs. Ouderkirk, a man who was hallucinating that his 70 year old wife was "entertaining men for immoral purposes" left her the sum of $5, stating that "he wanted to provide a good home for her". Maybe he was just a cheapskate, but clearly CRAZY! The courts upheld that he was "clearly delusional". YA THINK?

British law, the basis for most of our current laws, dealt with testamentary capacity in the famous case of Banks vs. Goodfellow in 1870. The British Court decided that the testator was indeed delusional, but it did not prevent him from understanding what he was doing with his will. Over the last 100 plus years, it hasn't changed much. It's still vague and its interpretation is filled with loopholes big enough to drive many trucks through.

The Journal of the American Academy of Psychiatry and the Law, in an article by Thomas Gutheil, MD, spells out some of the criteria needed to evaluate "testamentary capacity" in this general outline:

At the time of the execution of a will (which may include a lucid interval in a chronic disorder) a person must understand:

- the nature and extent of the assets and property of the estate;
- the natural heirs of his/her bounty (including actual persons such as relatives and friends, charities, organizations, and religious bodies, among others), whether any heir actually receives a bequest or receives nothing;
- the significance of a will as governing the distribution of property after the testator's death.

In some contexts, there is a fourth element that adds a deliberative aspect to "knowledge":

- the testator should have a rational plan for distribution of property after death.

The one phrase "lucid interval in a chronic disorder" is the BIGGEST PROBLEM OF THE TESTAMENTARY CAPACITY ARGUMENT. How can you be considered sane for one moment when basically you suffer from a mental chronic disorder? This vague interpretation by the courts leaves family members with justifiable claims basically no recourse. It is time for the laws to change.

Since it's no longer 1870, I think it's time to bring the law and modern technology into the 21st century. I suggest mandatory videotaping of the changing of any will or trust, so that a forensic psychiatrist can really examine the behavior of the person changing their will. In the video, the above criteria for the evaluation of mental capacity should be asked of them, and recorded to be studied at a later date if necessary. This way there will be less debate and less wide open speculative interpretation of "testamentary capacity". The video can be watched over and over to be analyzed.

This has the potential of stopping billions of dollars from being incorrectly distributed to undeserving family members, caretakers, recently married spouses, and just about any undeserving undesirable. WE NEED NEW LAWS to stop the thieves.

Chapter Seven

The Funeral: The Last Stop

When it comes to vultures coming out of the woodwork, there is nothing like a good old-fashioned funeral to bring them all out. It's like watching a Tennessee Williams play: everyone shows up ready to play their part. Some people genuinely reflect their grief, and cannot disguise their sadness, and some show up with the incomplete baggage of their relationship with the deceased. With the latter, you can feel the "mendacity" with every fiber of your being. Some people show up that you have never met, and you find out how they were involved with your parents. Neighbors, relatives, business associates, maybe even secret lovers come out of the woodwork. As they all enter the church or temple, they seem to assess each other as they walk in. It's interesting how people take their seats as well. The ones that think that they're going to be remembered in the will sit as close to the front as possible with the deceased's family, and those only there to pay their respects sit more towards the back, so that they can make a quick exit. That said, the solemn vibes of a funeral are overwhelming to most of us. Most of us feel nervous and sad when we attend them, never knowing exactly how to feel or what to say. To people who work in funeral parlors, however, it's just another day of cleaning up soiled tissues, and laying out the Bibles. These people prey upon your emotions during your most vulnerable time in your life, and they know it. The conversation at the funeral home usually sounds like this:

> "Surely your relative would want to be in a solid mahogany coffin, rather than pressboard!"

> "You don't want a plot that is right next to the bathroom or the freeway for eternity for them, do you? The one near the waterfall is not that much more in price!"

> "We give you five words to summarize your loved one in our package. Surely you have more to say about your relative than that!"

> "That'll be twenty thousand dollars. Would like to finance that? We have a reasonable monthly payment plan."

They are the most obvious of vultures, as they are literally the last stop. One thing's for sure, they have job security: no shortage of work, ever. They get all sorts of requests these days, as people are getting more creative about funerals. The funeral director told me of a woman who wanted to be buried in a pink coffin and her daughter wanted to play "Ding Dong the Witch is Dead" during her ceremony!

For my own father's funeral, he had bought the "Eternity" package before he died at a place called "Serenity Memorials", which included a very small bouquet (I've seen better ones on freeway onramps), a signature book with a picture of an American Eagle on it, and an urn that I could have sworn that I saw at the 99 cent store. Of course they showed us all of this rinky dink crap expecting us to upgrade. We didn't.

Because we decided not to upgrade, I knew I was in trouble when the sign for the service spelled our last name wrong, and the two workers wanted to come to our reception so that they could have a free lunch. We were in the middle of a trust war when my dad died, so everyone hated each other. The funeral was like watching a Fellini movie. Most of the people there were bussed in from the rest home that my dad had been in. They went from funeral to funeral because it was a chance to have something different than the canned spaghetti and jello that the rest home served.

The rest of the people who wandered in were dysfunctional family members, my brother's AA group, and my dad's two girlfriends, one being my aunt, and the other his next door neighbor at the rest home. Not surprising, Dick, the oh so kind attorney, and the skanky realtor who was in the process of selling my dad's house, also slithered in. My brother was wearing a bowling shirt, and his kids were wearing flip flops and looked like they were on their way to the beach. My brother's wife was dressed in black and white and looked like a waiter. I got it! She looked like Paul Prudhomme, the

New Orleans chef!

My brother's side of the family were really upset that my side of the family showed up. They were so close to writing me out of the Trust, they could taste it. The only problem-- my dad died suddenly, which seemed to ruin everyone's plan! The lawyer was really nervous-- he looked worried, and he had every reason to be: he had been spending trust money without any oversight from anyone for quite some time, and, NOT SO FAST, TONTO—he knew that the jig was up. Now that my father had died, he knew that he had to deal with ME. And here we were at the funeral…ONE BIG HAPPY FAMILY.

Next came the seating arrangements: I had to sit up front, which I could have skipped, next to my brother, which was uncomfortable to say the least. This pissed off my aunt, who thought that she had stepped in as our surrogate mother, and now there was no place in the front row for her to sit. Her only other option was to sit across the aisle next to my dad's rest home girlfriend, who she hated. What an insult! She was even wearing my mom's pink velour jumpsuit and her jewelry for the occasion!

Now came the speeches. The minister didn't have a clue as to who my father was, so he winged it by reciting basic passages from the Bible. Then he desperately asked, "Does anyone have anything to say?"

My brother stepped up to the podium in his bowling shirt, and pulled out a ten page speech. It went on and on and on. People started leaving. The AA people desperately looked around for a place to sneak and have a cigarette. Old friends of my dad's gave up on the free meal and left. The place started to empty out. My brother's eulogy had worn everyone out. The old people excused themselves to go to the bathroom. Some of the people from the rest home had already started to serve themselves in the other room. He finished the speech with a flourish, but no one was paying attention. I know I sound really callous about all of this, but the funeral was the end product of six years of dementia and trust wars. The whole thing was hypocritical to say the least, as most of the people involved in the memorial only knew my father the last few years of his life. In other words, they didn't know him at all.

Funerals really do bring out the best and worst in people. In the case of my grandfather's funeral, most of his friends were dead, and there weren't enough pallbearers to carry the casket, so my cousins, myself and my husband helped out (two women, and two middle aged men). Being a woman, I had never carried a casket, nor do I ever want to again, but in this case there was no choice. Our family was estranged (I'm sure you're not surprised by that), and not many people were left that associated with each other. My mother hadn't talked to her sister in ten years, and my grandfather had left a mess of his affairs. He had basically given my mother everything, leaving my aunt with five thousand dollars if she did not contest the will. Now after ten years of not speaking to each other, they were face to face over my grandfather's coffin. Needless to say, the coffin hadn't even been lowered and the family was already fighting. I felt like I was watching "The War Of The Roses": My uncle spit on the ground and pointed to the coffin and said "Dave was always a son of a bitch, cheap bastard." My aunt looked at my mother angrily and chimed in, "You turned Dad against me". The yelling and fighting continued for twenty minutes, as my cousin Frank and I viewed it from a distance. My cousin Frank looked at me and said "Look at these peasants--the body's not even buried and they are already at it".

It was true. My family were a bunch of peasants from Poland, and they wore their emotions on their sleeves. After the coffin finally made it into the ground, everyone got into their cars never to be seen again. That was the last of my grandparents and extended family. Basically my mother liquidated my grandfather's trust, and never gave my aunt anything--not even the photographs. Later I questioned my mother, and she replied to me " If I give it to her, there won't be anything left for you in the future." It turns out that my mother not only turned on my aunt, but also turned on me! She ended up writing me out of her will, as she felt I too, had "slighted her", just like my grandfather . Oh well, "like father like daughter".

Okay, so my family isn't exactly "The Waltons", but whose is? Sometimes a funeral can reflect the love and loss of an entire community for someone. I attended the funeral of a schoolteacher who was loved so much by the community that it overflowed the church and was held outside. She always had a fondness for wildlife, and especially birds, and even THEY showed up. As the choir was singing her favorite song, twenty parrots flew over and echoed the verse.

A funeral really tells us how someone lived their life and how they treated others. My friend Bart was so loved by the small town that he lived in that he had a line of cars a mile long waiting to park at the church the funeral was in. But his wife, on the other hand, only had immediate family at hers in the same church a few years later. No one knew her, even though she went to the church every Sunday and Bart never went!

Things can really get ugly when the person who died had remarried, and the kids from the previous marriage don't get along with them. My friend Caroline flew all the way to London for her father's funeral only to be turned away at the church door by her stepmother. When I was in Ireland, I visited a catacomb where a family crypt had very ornate coffins and one plain pine box. When I asked the curator what the story was, he explained that no one ever liked the guy in the pine box, and the family hated him so much that no one would ever be buried in the crypt again, as they didn't want to spend eternity next to him. There is nothing new about how people behave at funerals. It is the one last time that people can express their true feelings about that person....GOOD OR BAD.

Chapter Eight

Fallout

A death is like a bomb dropping on a family, and it takes time for everyone to crawl through the wreckage, pick up the pieces, and find their equilibrium again. After a relative has died, there is always a transition from being in the "fight or flight" mode to the "acceptance" and "clean up" mode. The best transitions occur when the person who died has made their wishes very clear, left their finances in order, and have a family will or trust that everyone has read and understood. This, of course, is a healthy family that communicates constantly and has had many a discussion on what happens when someone dies. On the other hand, a friend of mine told me that before his father died, he handed him and his brother a giant bill for all of the debts that he had incurred over the previous ten years, and asked them to take care of it! Not exactly "Father of the Year", but at least he was up-front about it! Unfortunately, many families get stuck with the bills when someone dies in their family. They may have to pay for funerals, outstanding nursing home costs—it can really get expensive. Family members that don't deal with what will happen to their belongings after their death usually have problems dealing with death, period. It IS unpleasant. It IS depressing. But if you don't deal with it, all of these problems are passed down to the heirs, and it can be living hell to settle an estate.

There are many pitfalls and traps all along the road to settling a trust, not to mention all of the vultures on the side of the road waiting for you to make a mistake. Some families think they are doing the right thing by appointing an attorney to act as a professional trustee, instead of having their family members act as one. WRONG! It's even worse if they are affiliated with a financial advisor or brokerage firm. These people know exactly how to make your family money disappear. Some professional trustees have an incentive to prolong the process of distributing the trust. They don't get caught ENOUGH, but when they do, it's jail time. An accountant, John Hibbard, dipped into a family trust fund and stole over $700,000 from it. He did it to keep his accountancy business afloat, and was gambling on an investment to bail him out of his hole. IT DIDN'T. He's now serving three years in prison, BUT THE FAMILY TRUST IS GONE, and it will never be back. SAYONARA! Many elderly people sign over a power of attorney to their trusted attorneys, hoping that they will interpret their wishes as opposed to a family member. The power of attorney, however, can be a license to STEAL. It puts the ultimate power over assets in the POA holder's hands. It is estimated that over a half million elderly people are ripped off this way by family members, lawyers and accountants to the tune of over 2.6 BILLION DOLLARS annually. Financial advisors for the elderly have been known to funnel their client's money to fake companies in order to steal their assets. It is essentially greed brought on by a sense of entitlement. A lot of times financially strapped siblings, even though the parents are still alive, may want their inheritance paid to them beforehand, their logic being that they are going to "Get it anyway". There are a million rationalizations. What they all have in common is GREED. If a power of attorney is necessary, especially when dementia or Alzheimer's is involved, try to split the POA between siblings so that at least there is some accountability involved.

It is imperative that you communicate with your parents while they are alive and of sound mind in regard to what goes to whom, where they want to be buried, and who should be trustees. It is a must to have communication with your family at least every six months while everyone is alive. This, as unpleasant a task as it is, will help you in the long run. If you can get all of your family to cooperate in this task, there won't be any ugly surprises. If you are planning on leaving certain assets to one particular person, tell everyone now, AND TELL THEM WHY.

Another word of advice: GO THROUGH YOUR FAMILY TRUST WITH A FINE TOOTH COMB. I heard from an attorney how he was going through the old trust of a new client, looking to see how he could update it for him. As he went over it, he found two people set to receive $30,000 apiece. At his next meeting, he asked the new client who the people were. HE HAD NO IDEA! It turned out that the sloppy previous attorney had probably cut and pasted something from SOMEONE ELSE'S TRUST INTO HIS CLIENT'S!

Unfortunately, most of us don't know anything about our parent's family trust until it is too late. In my case, I felt like I inherited a sinking barge of garbage. The barge was filled with financial problems, a crooked attorney, dysfunctional family members, and rotten contracts signed with my father while he had dementia. It was basically a new full time job of shoveling up other people's crap WITH NO PAY.

After my family funeral drama died down, it was time to do the meeting with the lawyer to see what was really going on with the trust or will. My brother and I met with Dick, the oh so kind attorney, and he told us that we were splitting everything 50-50. A few weeks later, he called us in for another meeting (at $350 an hour) and told us that he was WRONG in the first meeting. Mind you, he himself had written the Trust, and didn't understand it! You see how this works? He was ringing up a tab! He then reread the Trust and found that there were actually two trusts going on, an irrevocable (meaning written in stone—can't be changed) that was in play after my mother died, and gave large portions to be held in trust for the grandchildren. Of course, this left my brother and I with significantly less from the estate, and of course, since my brother had already scammed my father out of $300,000, there wasn't much cash left. So after Dick, the oh so kind attorney, had scammed us out of more hours for his ever growing timekeeper summary, what this really meant was that we needed to sell my parent's home to get whatever we could out of it. Knowing that my deadbeat brother would probably be too scatterbrained to help out on the task, I was beginning to realize that "inheritance" didn't just mean money, it also meant WORK WITHOUT PAY.

The worst part about it was that I had to deal with my brother for every financial decision that was to be made about the house. The first place to start, I believed, was to get rid of the scumbag neighbor realtor that my father had signed with to sell the house. He was getting a 6% commission, wasn't affiliated with any realty firm, and had one listing: MY DAD'S HOUSE! Dick, the oh so kind attorney, wanted us to meet with the realtor in his office, of course, and charge us for it, because he was friends with him and probably getting a piece of the action. Being a rat himself, my brother must've smelled a relative, because he let me go ahead and fire the realtor. Here is my email to him:

Jim and Tammy,

We appreciate the relationship you had with our father, and we thank you for your previous involvement of the home for sale.

At this time we both feel we should be free to explore all of our options. We have both decided that we will not require your services as realtors or rental agents, and we respectfully decline your offer to rent our home for your son's conference.

At this point, we want no one to enter the house. Please

return any keys you may have to one of the guards at the guard gate as soon as possible. We will be down in a couple of weeks to let you in and allow you to take out the furnishings that you loaned to our father to stage the home.

Sincerely,

Katherine and Robbie Steel

Of course, they disobeyed our order to not enter the home, brought a moving van and God knows what they took out of the house. I wrote them an email telling them if I found anything missing, I would report it to the police. I got this back:

From: Jim and Tammy

Katherine,

To suggest that we are liable for anything missing is shocking, saddening and insulting. Neither of us have any desire to have further contact with you, Katherine. Whatever valuables that were locked have been untouched by us, and the furniture items in the garage your dad went over with Robbie were untouched as you will see. Tammy did not go into the garage yesterday. The home is yours and your responsibility.

Jim and Tammy

What's worse is that he told my crazy aunt, who they were now BFFs with. She sent my brother and I this email:

> From: Aunt Deedee
>
> Robbie, I have no problem with your wanting others to be in on the sale if you can get them. I find it most annoying that you don't feel that I should be made aware of this. What I do find extremely upsetting are the accusations leveled by Katherine towards Jim and Tammy. This is extremely unacceptable towards a very honest couple of friends. Shame on you, Katherine! Your mother would be horrified! (actually my mother didn't like her sister *or* these people)

At this point, I'd finally had it with all of them. For years they demonized me for wanting to take responsibility for my dad's affairs while they sponged off of him. Enough was enough. I wrote her this back:

> Aunt Deedee,
>
> The selling of our parent's house has absolutely nothing to do with you. My parents left nothing in their trust to you, and no mention of you whatsoever. Our home, and what we choose to do with it, is not your business.
>
> Katherine

In essence, f**k off. For some reason, it didn't feel that great to get rid of these bloodsucking leeches. I knew deep down that whatever they took from us they got away with. I consider myself one of the lucky people compared to a 98-year-old woman and her mentally disabled daughter, both of whom lived alone in a beautiful old home. The two women were embraced by guess what? A KINDLY COUPLE that lived next door. The kindly neighbors somehow talked the elderly lady into giving them the title to her property, valued at $1.1 million. They then took a mortgage against the property in order to acquire funds to make improvements on their own home and take vacations. They then directed her to their friends, who were financial advisors, and they succeeded in depleting the elderly woman's financial resources by moving her cash into expensive annuities carrying attractive commissions and fees for the sales agents, together with deep penalties for early liquidation.

Luckily for the elderly lady, her deceased sister's accountant became involved after settling her sister's estate. He offered to help the elderly lady with her finances, and discovered all of the wrongdoing when he investigated her assets. He advised her to get an attorney. The case never went to trial.

In the settlement that was reached, the deed to the elderly woman's home was given back to her, and $1 million in cash was returned to the estate by the various financial advisers who participated in the issuance of the annuities. The defendants denied any wrongdoing, and weren't prosecuted. They ended up with $150,000 of the elderly woman's money as a settlement for "the years of caretaking" that they had done.

It's the kind of story that is happening all too often to vulnerable grannies and grandpas. People are broke and trolling for bucks, and stealing from them is like taking candy from a baby.

AGAIN, BEWARE OF THE KINDLY NEIGHBORS.

Cleaning up the fallout after your parent's death also includes going through their bank statements, checking accounts, and paying all of the remaining bills. When going through my dad's checkbook, I was shocked to find page after page written to charities to the total of $10,000. Mind you, my father was not a generous guy. HE THOUGHT THAT THEY WERE BILLS THAT NEEDED TO BE PAID! He was always complaining about how many bills he had to pay, and I finally found out why—HIS DEMENTIA. I also found out that he had taken his Rolex watch to a pawnbroker and sold it to him for $500 because "he needed the money", which of course, he didn't. At least he made the pawnbroker happy. Dementia means FREE MONEY to the thousands of unscrupulous people that prey on the elderly. Some of them are televangelists that scare them into sending them money, some go door to door, and some do it through the mail. Some, like the following couple, did it through their radio program:

Kenneth Powell and Katie Rose hosted the "Ken and Katie" radio program that featured infomercials such as "Academy of Real Estate" and Money Intelligence" on a Ventura, California radio station. This is where they attracted the investors who ultimately became victims. Between them they swindled over 7 million dollars out of listeners, after promising them that they were developing property in Taft, California. It is one of the largest real estate fraud cases yet. Katie faces a sentence of 12 years for her crimes and Ken faces up to 18 years. None of the money that they embezzled can be found, and the victims aren't expected to be paid back. It's really a shame when people that scrimped and saved their entire lives fall victims to vultures that prey on the elderly. All I can say is that I'm glad my dad didn't live in Ventura.

Chapter Nine

My Lawyer vs. Your Lawyer

What's the difference between a lawyer and a vulture? A lawyer can take off his wingtips!

This chapter deals with the TRUE nitty-gritty, the stuff that trust wars are made of: the fight over money. Most of today's families fight over money because the previous generation saved money, and the new generation of inheritors has been used to spending and is mortgaged to the hilt. A friend of mine told me that he heard there are two types of behavior for heirs of trusts these days: "Waiters", and "Wishers". "Waiters" are the heirs that have been waiting for years to inherit money, banking on it, so to speak, to bail them out of debt. A "Wisher" on the other hand, is an heir that is so much in debt that they WISH THEIR PARENTS WOULD DIE so that they can get the money!

It takes a death in the family for siblings to really find out their true feelings about each other. As far as my family situation, I fall into the "hate" category. I don't care how wealthy any heir is, it is hard to ignore a family member that sucked $300,000 from your parent's 401k! Ouch. As you can tell from my writing style, that huge sum of money definitely created a rift between my brother and I. Now that our father had passed on to the big retirement home in the sky, we again returned to Dick, the oh so kind attorney's office to try and work out a deal. My brother, being the passive aggressive snake that he is, agreed to everything. Yes, he accepted the fact that he had taken more money than me. Yes, he knew that he should "equalize" the estate with me. And yes, he planned on doing it with me. When confronted with a document to sign stating he would equalize the $300,000 with me, he told us that he needed time to think about it, but OF COURSE WE WOULD SETTLE AT A LATER DATE, which never happened. He didn't return calls or emails and was essentially MIA after that.

I decided to orchestrate a "friendly' meeting with him outside the attorney's office to get him to come up with a settlement agreement. We met several times at the Denny's where he attended his AA meetings. Filled with the confidence that one gets from being the most sober in a roomful of losers, my brother, over his plate of waffles, informed me that "of course we would settle", it was #8 of the twelve steps—making reparations to those that you hurt during your addiction. We shook on it, and as we were leaving the place, all of the waiters and busboys at Denny's said goodbye to him—he was a popular client of theirs. A LOT OF AA MEETINGS, I guess.

Weeks went by and no more returned calls or emails. What happened to #8 OF THE TWELVE STEPS? I decided to try a meeting at a coffee house--neutral territory--to approach the equalization with him. This time, my tone wasn't so conciliatory. I was pissed. I asked him again to sign the equalization agreement. He hemmed and hawed, and wouldn't look me in the eye. I couldn't stand his wimpy non-committal behavior anymore, and I yelled at him about what a scumbag he was for sponging and embezzling all of the money from our mother and father. I told him that I would hold up the disbursement of trust monies from our dad's estate by not signing anything until he agreed to sign it. He looked at me through dazed eyes, as if he was on Prozac or something. He puffed out his chest like a rooster, and told me that "he didn't take kindly to threats!" He then stormed out of the place.

Weeks went by, papers came from the attorney, and I didn't sign them. He started to panic because he wanted the money so badly. He then hired an attorney to come after me. I don't know if you've heard the term "heart attack" letter: it refers to opening up your mailbox to find really disturbing, legally threatening letters that are meant to scare the crap out of you. The first one that they sent me looked like this (I've shortened it to show you the most toxic moments):

NOTICE TO NEGOTIATE

To: Katherine Steel

RE: Steel Revocable Trust

<u>**Under section 2, subsection B, article 3 of the STEEL**</u>

> **REVOCABLE TRUST, you are hearby notified of a meeting to negotiate the terms of the trust.** Please make an appointment to meet at the offices of Greenbaum and Greenbaum on the following date: January 27, 2011. **Recognize that it not outside the realm of possibilities that you could be removed in your position as co-trustee if you do not cooperate with the terms of the trust.**

As I said, this is the standard format of the "heart attack" letter. Bold print. Underlined text. Quotes from laws. It went on for four or five pages of chest beating and saber rattling threats. The letter's intent was to intimidate me into going to an attorney to translate the document for me, which, of course, I did. He wasn't impressed, and translated it for me. Essentially, she was using a clause of the Trust to get me to come in and mediate with my brother, which would have been fine if the rest of the five pages hadn't essentially outlined the position that my brother did not have to equalize with me, as the money he took was a "gift", and not a "loan". In other words, he had no intention of giving any of the money that he took back to any of the beneficiaries.

Under my lawyer's counsel, I returned with the following email, pretending that I wrote it and did not have an attorney. We also did not underline or embolden any type to make it more matter-of-fact, and "ho-hum" in tone:

> Dear Ms. Greenbaum,
>
> I am glad to hear that your client and my brother Robbie Jr. intend to follow the exact provisions of the trust. As trustees, Robbie Jr. and I both owe each other fiduciary duties. We also have the obligation as beneficiaries,

along with the other beneficiaries, to fund the ongoing operating expenses of the Trust given the Trust is illiquid.

In order to perform our respective fiduciary duties I have been requesting all of the Trust's documents from Dick. I am concerned with Dick's control of the Trust over the last three years and the extensive fees Dick was paid by the Trust. Until I have received and reviewed the Trust's files, I cannot reach any conclusions on this issue. It is my hope that Robbie Jr. will participate in collecting the Trust's documents, reviewing them, and then taking appropriate action to recover Trust assets.

The Trust is not liquid. My concern about this was part of the reason I was hesitant to distribute our respective shares of the assets. I look forward to working with Robbie Jr. and you to wrap up the affairs of the Trust expeditiously.

Sincerely,

Katherine Steel
Co-Trustee

By not taking her threats seriously, and by not claiming to have counsel, my letter left her looking like a bully. We wanted to make the whole battle look like I was being attacked without representation, in case we had to go to court. It was also a game my attorney wanted to play to make my brother spend more money. It worked, because they did not like the letter, and came back with another five page "heart attack" letter entitled:

RENEWED NEGOTIATION NOTICE

To: Katherine Steel

RE: Steel Revocable Trust

As stated in G&G INC's March 11th letter, <u>there are no outstanding loans that Robbie Jr. or his children owe either the Estate of Robert Steel.</u> Therefore, the only remaining asset of the TRUST is your father's house ("HOUSE'), which must be sold and the proceeds thereof distributed pursuant to the provisions of the TRUST. Specifically, Robbie Jr. does not share your belief that anything untoward occurred with regard to the services provided to your parents by Counsel who has represented your parents for at least the last two decades. While you and Robbie Jr. jointly hold the office of Trustee both of you are required to act together to administer the TRUST. While many of the questions you ask are ripe for discussion in a meeting, and Robbie Jr. is willing to discuss same with you at such a meeting, Robbie Jr. has no obligation to obtain the answer to your many questions.

Blah ba-blah blah. It also threatened arbitration, told me that I wasn't performing my duties as trustee, told me that the arbitrator might decide against me, and again insisted that my brother owed no money to the trust. It gave me three "ultimatums" that it insisted I address. My attorney then told me to respond to this letter with a passive/aggressive tone, still ringing up my brother's tab by making Ms. Greenbaum more and more angry and verbose:

Dear Ms. Greenbaum,

Your three "Ultimatums" appear to be determined to create disputes where none exist.

1. I agree we should list the house for sale.

2. I agree that the Trust should pay outstanding expenses. However, I still believe the Trust should contest some of Dick, the oh so kind attorney's invoices.

3. All beneficiaries (not just Robbie Jr. and me) need to advance funds to pay the Trust's expenses.

4. I disagree with Robbie Jr.'s assertion that we have "all records pertaining to the Trust." Even a quick glance of the documents provided indicates that many documents are missing. Robbie Jr.'s "confusion" over the need to collect all Trust documents, not just the Trust agreement and amendments, indicates his unwillingness to perform his fiduciary obligations to the Trust beneficiaries. While I understand why Robbie Jr. might be motivated to this, he is breaching his fiduciary duties to the Trust and all of its beneficiaries if he insists on proceeding without collecting all relevant documents and determining the correct characterization (gift v. loan) of all amounts the Trust paid Robbie Jr.

I am disappointed that Robbie Jr. believes we are now adversaries. It appears that the only potential disputes we may have relate to (1) The collection of all Trust documents; and (2) Characterizing payments to Robbie Jr. as gifts or loans. If Robbie Jr. is refusing to collect all Trust documents now, there is a dispute between the parties and we should proceed with a negotiation under subsection 6 of the Appendix to the Trust. Please advise if Robbie Jr. is refusing to collect all Trust documents. If this is the case, I will obviously need to engage counsel to attend the meeting with me. When the meeting occurs will be impacted by my counsel's availability. I look forward to your responses to all of the above questions and issues.

Sincerely,

Katherine Steel

This form of communication went on for a month. It was stressful receiving each "heart attack" letter, but my attorney enjoyed playing this game with them. He got a lot of delight pushing Ms. Greenbaum's buttons this way, which made her write more and more. I was happy to hear that my brother was paying a lot of money to the attorney that he hired. It made me feel all warm and fuzzy inside to know that he was finally getting back some of the aggravation that he had caused me over the years.

This is the point where attorneys really start focusing in for the kill. They know that it's going to be a long bumpy ride, with lots of fighting, which equals lots of money. The emails, letters, complaints, et cetera, all cost money on the infamous "timekeeper summary". We were officially now in the email wars of "My Lawyer vs. your Lawyer". Every correspondence was now cc'd to everyone's email. It made everyone accountable in print, with a legal file for backup. Cost aside, this turned out to be the only way to handle my brother. He would never respond to my emails before, and now he had to because Ms. Greenbaum was copied on my correspondence. She was like his surrogate mother. A SURROGATE JEWISH MOTHER! In other words, he'd better pay attention, OR ELSE!

WHAT DID I LEARN FROM THIS? If you have a dysfunctional family member that won't deal, hire a lawyer. It will light a fire under their ass to DO SOMETHING.

The months of heart attack letters finally stopped when we agreed to meet at Ms. Greenbaum's office. My lawyer and I met in the lobby, and then went up the elevator to the office. When we entered the office, Ms. Greenbaum, a slightly built, no-nonsense woman who had moved to San Francisco from New York recently, led me into a room where she had me sit by myself. She told me that my brother was sitting in another room, and that she and my attorney were going to discuss our case first, then bring us all together. Time went by. It was like sitting in a dentist's office, knowing that in a few minutes you were going to be drilled. My attorney came in with a big smile on his face. He told me that my brother had told Ms. Greenbaum that I had a violent temper and that he had warned her to expect angry outbursts. This is a 6'2" 300 pound man telling her this. Apparently, Ms. Greenbaum was under the impression that I was one CRAZY BITCH! My attorney liked it that way. He told me to act really civil and polite, and make Ms. Greenbaum understand that I WAS THE SANE ONE.

We went into the room, and everyone, including myself, was wearing corporate attire. After all, it is AN ATTORNEY'S OFFICE! My brother, however, was wearing one of his XXL hawaiian shirts. He looked like a bad lighting fixture in a tiki bar. He also looked scared. Or maybe it was guilt. We met the other GREENBAUM, who was Ms. Greenbaum's husband. He started talking sports talk to us, like "How about those Giants?" and "Are you a Warriors fan?" I looked around the office. My lawyer was $350 an hour. God knows what the Greenbaums were charging my brother. But I got the drill. They were running the clock to pad their timekeeper summaries by making a bunch of inane small talk about sports and the like. I finally said "Aren't we supposed to be having a meeting?" to the other Greenbaum, who got that it was time to go. Nice try, Mr. Greenbaum.

At this point, my brother was ready to crap his pants, he was so nervous. He always had trouble confronting people, but this was getting ridiculous. Ms. Greenbaum handed out an agenda of what we were supposed to talk about, and we started the blow by blow process of dealing with all of the outstanding issues from the "heart attack" letters. Each subject was dealt with, disagreed with, and basically left unsettled. Neither my brother or I were happy with the final outcome of the meeting: all it did was just kick the can down the road to be dealt with later on. One thing it did settle was that we agreed to list my parent's house for sale, and deposit money into a trust account so that we could pay bills. I insisted on being the signatory on the account, as I didn't trust my brother with the money (you think?). So, a couple thousand dollars later, we were no closer to working things out. I still hated him for taking $300,000 of the family trust.

It looked like we were facing many more meetings and timekeeper summaries before we settled anything.

Our sibling feud over $300,000 is chump change compared to the Koch brothers feud, whose estate was worth $5.6 billion and the amount contested was $2.3 billion. The four sons of Fred Koch, co-founder of energy conglomerate Koch Industries, spent nearly twenty years feuding with one another over whether two brothers, Charles and David, cheated the other two, William and Frederick, out of $2.3 billion when they sold their shares of Koch Industries in 1983 for around $1 billion. For years, the billionaires reportedly communicated only through lawyers, occasionally making efforts to publicly humiliate and discredit one another. After years of fighting and millions of dollars spent on legal fees, the brothers reconciled in 2001. Imagine what those timekeeper summaries looked like! Again, the only real winners WERE THE ATTORNEYS.

Some sibling inheritance feuds can get downright UGLY. Two brothers in Brooklyn, Tom Athanasatos, and his brother James, had been feuding since at least 1974 when Tom's marriage fell apart and he moved into his mother's home. He continued to live in the home after their mother died several years later, but he and his brother inherited the home equally from their mother's estate. Tom wanted to remain in the home, but James wanted to sell the home and split the proceeds. In a brotherly gesture, Tom invited James to come over to the house to work things out. They got into an argument instead. It got so bad that Tom went and got his homemade pellet gun and shot his brother in an attempt to kill him. Instead, he got his brother in the eye, blinding him!

Tom was so upset that he blinded his brother that he then put the pellet gun to his head, AND KILLED HIMSELF!

Emotions run high in dealing with family members over an estate. You don't want to end up on the wrong side of a pellet gun. Sometimes, unfortunately, you have to bite the bullet, and accept the fact that it is going to be MY LAWYER VS. YOUR LAWYER.

Chapter Ten

Trustee, Like It or Not

I have a neighbor where I live who was running for our homeowner's association presidency. On her application was a line where the candidate is supposed to write experience, and she wrote "Trustee". It is an important sounding word, isn't it? Makes you visualize men in business suits sitting in penthouse offices overlooking Manhattan. The exact definition goes something like this: a trustee or executor is a "fiduciary" of the estate and the beneficiaries of the will or trust. A fiduciary is someone who has a special duty of trust and responsibility to an individual or a group, such as the beneficiaries of a will or trust. Unfortunately, for most of us, being a trustee is very much like being the homeowner's association president: at the end of the day, you've basically been elected to clean up someone else's mess. Of course, the difference between trustee and homeowner's president is that you never really signed up for the position. You justify it, of course, because there is money involved, but it is time-consuming, aggravating, and the worst of it: if you don't do it correctly, the beneficiaries can SUE YOU! Being a trustee of someone else's estate, usually your parents, is like reading a book backwards. You think you're already at the end, but you have to start to read the previous pages to see what THE HELL HAPPENED.

When you've been chosen to act as the trustee of a trust, it's not just distributing the money you have to worry about: you have to worry about the people that you have to deal with as beneficiaries. The money is easy, compared to your wacky relatives. Your job will be a lot less stressful if you have a civil relationship with them, and are transparent with them about how you are handling the trust. They are almost always going to be anxious about their lack of control. If you follow the steps listed below, your dealings with them should be simpler:

> 1/Get in touch with the beneficiaries early.

> 2/Educate them about your role.

> 3/Help them to form realistic expectations of how long it will take to administer the trust, and how much they will receive.

> 4/Treat their questions as opportunities to engage them rather than as annoying intrusions.

> 5/Don't hide the trust document or assets from them.

The mistake that my father made was keeping everyone in the dark about his family trust, and making his attorney one of the successor trustees. My dad never discussed his trust to any of the beneficiaries, and when he was hit with Alzheimer's, we were totally reliant on the actions of his attorney, who left us in the dark as to what was happening with it. Because the attorney hid things from us, was secretive with trust documents, and allowed my father to remain as trustee even though he had trouble figuring out which way his pants were buttoned, as a beneficiary of the estate, and successor trustee, I was scared that his trust was being liquidated without being able to do anything about it. I was right. That was EXACTLY what was happening.

A trustee is actually required by law to keep beneficiaries reasonably informed about how they are managing the trust assets. Some states require that the trustee send specific kinds of notices and information to the beneficiaries on a regular basis. Check your local laws about this. These notices are a good idea, anyway, as they really are the minimum that they should be doing for the beneficiaries. If a trustee is upfront about where the money is and how it is invested, then there will be a lot less questions, challenges, and even potential lawsuits.

When a trustee keeps a beneficiary in the dark, suspicions start. They are usually warranted, as in the case of a friend of mine, whose sister was the trustee and conservator of his mother, who had dementia. Because his sister was secretive about the estate, he filed a petition in probate court that his sister had never provided an annual accounting to his mother. Because of this lack of accounting, he felt that his sister was taking advantage of his mother. He had the same problems with probate that I had. It took him five months to hear from the investigator that they had found some mismanagement, but probate still thought that his sister should remain as trustee. He probably had the same investigator I did who was too busy waiting for his coffee break to do his work!

When he asked for a copy of the report, he found that the only way that he could read it was through the discovery process if he filed for conservatorship. What he did find, though, was that his sister, the trustee, had spent over $100,000 of his mother's trust money defending herself on this with the attorney she had hired. He then found out that the court appointed attorney charged his mother's trust $10,000 for his report! Ouch!

In other words, probate cost him money and went nowhere. The worst of it was that his sister took money from the trust and paid a lawyer to threaten him with a $250,000 lawsuit if he proceeded any further with it. The attorney that she hired wanted him to sign a document that stated he would not pursue an accounting of the trust, otherwise they would have him "disinherited" under the grounds that he was challenging the trust. NOT A HAPPY ENDING. Double-death: his sister was using up the trust monies on attorney's fees to fight him, and legally BLACKMAILING him, to boot. When his mother finally died, there wasn't much left. Same old story: rotten sibling and greedy attorneys got it all.

Even though he was in the right, and his sister was obviously stealing, he needed to weigh out the cost of the lawyers and court costs before he started the process of probate. He needed to decide if it was really WORTH IT. When it comes to the law, it is not about being fair or honest, it's about how much money you are willing to spend, and how far you want to take it. It's like the lawyer joke:

What's the difference between a tick and a lawyer? A tick falls off of you when you die!

That said, as a trustee, you do not want to go down that road. You want to avoid litigation like the BLACK PLAGUE. If you follow these rules to the letter, you will be able to avoid most trustee nightmares. Think of Charlton Heston receiving the Ten Commandments on Mt. Sinai—these should be written in stone:

A Trustee may not receive a personal benefit from a transaction or decision. The Trustee administers the trust solely in the interest of the beneficiaries. A Trustee may not engage in self-dealing without court approval.

The Trustee has a duty to treat all beneficiaries impartially except when the terms of the trust provide otherwise. Accordingly, the Trustee should be even-handed in the Trustee's dealings with all of the beneficiaries.

The Trustee has a duty to keep trust property separate from other property. The Trustee is prohibited from commingling trust property with the Trustee's own property.

The Trustee has a duty to protect the trust property from loss or damage. The Trustee should not engage in speculative investing.

The Trustee has a duty to convert unproductive property to productive property.

The Trustee has a duty to distribute income to the trust beneficiaries in reasonable intervals during the term of the trust.

The Trustee has a duty to keep clear and accurate accounts showing in detail the nature and value of all the trust property and how the property has been administered, in addition to a duty to satisfy a beneficiary's reasonable requests for information.

The Trustee has a duty to use reasonable efforts to enforce the trust's claims.

The Trustee has a duty to take reasonable steps to defend the trust property against the claims and actions of others.

Assets of trusts come in many forms: money, homes, stocks, land, et cetera. Sometimes the only asset is a home that needs to be divided among many people. That's when things get STICKY. Not only do you have to sell the property, you have to keep it up while having it on the market. You have to get a realtor that every one agrees on, and basically all decisions have to go through the other trustees.

For example, most of my parent's estate was in their house, which was vacant and for sale for a year. Because it was being shown by realtors, it needed to look nice, so it still needed to have a gardener. I DIDN'T EVEN HAVE A GARDENER! It also still needed a maid to keep the dust down and open up the windows every two weeks. I DIDN'T HAVE A MAID, EITHER! Every Monday I wrote checks to people I'd never met out of a joint account with my brother. Since our trust was left "illiquid", meaning that my brother and I, as co-trustees, did not have any operating expenses, we were forced to subsidize the home by digging into our own pockets every few months to pay for homeowner's fees, gas, electric, gardeners, maids, taxes-- you name it. I was made the signatory on the account by the attorneys, since my brother's credibility was DUBIOUS, TO SAY THE LEAST. The original realtor that my brother and his attorney picked was terrible, so six months went by without an offer. She was such a terrible realtor I kept expecting a classified in Craigslist of the house next to an ad for "Garage Sales". She put the house in all of the throw-away papers in San Rafael, and I mean throwaway. I'm sure that the only people that read the ad were probably homeless and sleeping on it! On her emails to us, her portrait was actually bigger than the picture of the house, making all of us wonder what she was actually selling—her ego or our house! I was after her for months to get an ad into a "showcase" style home magazine—"Dream Homes of San Rafael". She finally sent me the miserable magazine that she put it in, and it was surrounded by houses in Redding! It also had the wrong information on it. We had to get a new realtor, but my brother was MIA. Two weeks of endless emails to him and his attorney finally allowed me to start interviewing new realtors. The whole process took a month, not to mention bills from my own attorney who had to read all of their stupid emails. I found a realtor that had a great track record, but NO. More emails were necessary to review her contract and bring her on board. ANOTHER TWO WEEKS! You see where I'm going with this? Being a trustee takes the patience of MOTHER TERESA. I could almost see blood coming from my palms.

After months of negotiations we finally ended up selling our home. This was monumental, as I could see a light in at the end of the tunnel. I began to think I was nearing the home stretch of this miserable process.

Chapter Eleven

Who Gets What

Okay, so the family house has finally sold, and there's finally money and family possessions to be distributed. You are relieved that you're not spending money on it anymore, and the trust assets are finally LIQUID. This is when you are introduced to even more emotional rollercoasters and legal chicanery. In my case, the escrow on the house wasn't too painful, but it was tricky because the estate had been split into TWO TRUSTS: The Steel Survivor Trust, and The Grandchildren Trust. Funds from escrow, then, went into these two trusts, divided in a 40/60 split of shares. Weird, but according to the miserable trust that Dick, the oh so kind attorney, had sold my father, that was what we were stuck with. We painfully negotiated these financial rapids with both my brother's and my own attorney steering the way. You got it: Cha-ching! More money for the attorneys—more bites out of the family whale. Understanding the math that calculated the division of funds required more than eighth grade algebra to understand —The Steel Survivor Trust (40%) was split by my brother and I, and the Grandchildren's Trust was divided in an exceptionally wacky manner with my brother and I each getting 25% of THAT, then the kids splitting up the remaining 50% three ways. On top of that, the Grandchildren Trust stipulated that they get disbursements of what was left at their 25th, 30th, and 35th birthdays, but only if they were sober and submitted to drug testing (I guess my father put that one in because of my brother!). Since this was my final opportunity to get out of any financial dealings with my brother and his family, we had the lawyers split up the trusts, and create new ones for EACH FAMILY. Again, Cha-CHING! More money for the attorneys. The family whale kept getting smaller and smaller. Add taxes to that—the kids all had to pay an exorbitant property tax rate in the State of California, which all had to be calculated by—you guessed it: cha-CHING! Accountants!

You'd think that watching this horrifying spectacle of your inheritance being whittled away by attorneys and taxes would be enough for me, but NO. I felt like I still had a chance trying to recoup some of the GIANT BITES that my brother had taken out of the whale before we got into this mess. I dug through letter after letter of correspondence from my dad to him, trying to find the magic word "loan", which brings us to the other exasperating part of inheritance battles: GIFT vs. LOAN. If your scumbag sibling asks your parent for money, and says that they will pay them back, that is essentially a loan. My brother asked for so much money from my parents that he essentially gave up on that tactic, as everyone knew that he would never pay them back. I did find a few letters from him promising to pay some loans back, and a letter from my dad promising a school that he would loan my brother $5000 a month for six months so that he could attend. Armed with these letters, I took them to my attorney, and told him to duke it out with Ms. Greenbaum, my brother's attorney. We reversed the saber rattling and threatened THEM with mediation this time. We also threatened a suit so that we could subpoena Dick, the oh so kind attorney, for the Trust files. It began a slow, sluggish stink war that eventually worked into a compromise. My brother did not want us to get into the docs that Dick, the oh so kind attorney had, so he agreed to pay back some money to the trust out of his proceeds. We settled on a figure of $80,000, which was a really sad compromise from $300,000. To tell you the truth, I was so beaten up from the whole experience, I just wanted it to end. Since he had taken the loan before the "Survivor Trust" kicked in, I had to split the award with the kids, which brought my share down. Better than a stick in eye, I guess, but it hardly paid for all of the aggravation that he had caused me. So, in essence, we split up the funds over a period of several months, and of course, it was nowhere near what everyone expected to get. There was a lot of complaining on both sides, but I was so done with it, I was happy it was over.

If you really look at most trust distributions, I actually had it pretty easy. Families are complicated. At least I was lucky enough to have parents that stayed married until the end....although my dad looked like he was getting offers from Aunt DeeDee and his rest home neighbor! When new marriages happen, there can be some pretty huge battles, like the estate of the co-founder of Johnson and Johnson, John Seward Johnson I. When he died, he left his entire fortune to his third wife, who was his former maid and 42 years younger than him! Three years and $10 million in legal fees later, a judge found that Johnson had not been mentally competent when he signed his will, and ordered her to pay Johnson's children $160 million.

Sometimes the grandchildren are the ones to raise a stink, as in the case of H.L. Hunt. He was at one point among the richest men in the United States, with a large number of trusts to provide for his family. In 2008, H.L.'s first great-grandchild, Albert G. Hill III, sued his father, sisters, aunts and Tom Hunt, H.L.'s nephew, claiming they were mismanaging his grandmother and great uncle's trust funds, along with their primary asset, Hunt Petroleum. The dispute came to a head when Tom Hunt, who was chairman of Hunt Petroleum at the time, decided to sell the company. The stink shifted back to the grandson, because Albert III was eventually disinherited. Ouch. BIG OUCH. MILLIONS OF DOLLARS OUCH. He was cut out of the family business, and Hunt Petroleum was sold. After his disinheritance, Albert III's life really went south. He and his wife were indicted on multiple felony counts of mortgage fraud, arising after the couple lied about their income to obtain a home improvement loan.

We all understand why people fight over money. After all, it IS the root of all evil. Or, LACK OF IT is the root of all evil, which seems to be more accurate. Money is power, money is freedom, and money in the bank makes you feel a lot better about your situation. There is no denying it. But what happens to all of the knick knacks your parents have collected over the years? The old clock your grandmother had. Mom's wedding ring. Your dad's gun/pipe/stamp collection. Epic fights can happen over these items. You may be able to cut up the stamp collection. You can make copies of the photos. You can't however, cut an antique watch in half, or your mother's wedding ring. In these fights, SOMEONE, OR SOMETHING HAS TO GIVE!

It went like this: for some reason everyone wanted my mom's sofa that she had inherited from her parents. Even wacky Aunt DeeDee wanted it. I didn't even like it, but I pretended that I wanted it just to have leverage with them about the stuff that I really WANTED. After all of the crap my brother and his miserable family had put me through, it was time for me to turn the knife a bit. I was a stickler about everything, even though I was ready to take most of the stuff to Goodwill. It absolutely amazed me the capacity of greed that my brother and his wife had towards all the weird collection of stuff that my parents collected over the years. They wanted everything, even the paper napkins. I was surprised that they didn't take the wallpaper off of the walls! Actually, the few times that I had visited their house for holiday dinners, it struck me that they were huge hoarders: stacks of newspapers and crap everywhere, a garage filled with so much garbage you couldn't even enter it, and overflowing cat litter boxes from the four cats they had. I finally stopped going to their house for family functions when I watched them let their cat walk from the cat box onto a table full of food and lick a plate of butter. My family even had a song: "I'm dreaming of a cat box Christmas….just like the one I used to know…."

Cat boxes aside, I still had to deal with my brother and his dysfunctional family when we had to divvy up my parent's belongings. I was way ahead of the distribution of them, because luckily I had gone to my father's house years earlier to photograph and videotape his belongings at his request. I did a very detailed accounting of his belongings, room by room, down to the towels and silverware.

The lawyers told us that the only family members to be at the house to divide the belongings were my brother and I. NO SPOUSES. For good reason. Not only did this spare me the visual nightmare of looking at his wife, it also spared us a trip to the ER, as emotions were high and my brother's wife may have ended up there if she kept mouthing off to me.

When my brother and I arrived at the house, I noticed that quite a few things were missing. My brother wasn't aware that I had done a photo inventory, and was trying to convince me that Dad never owned certain items that I claimed he had. I brought out my computer. A picture is worth a thousand words. I said I DARE NOT ROBBIE JR., take a look. Robbie Jr. looked stunned. I suggested that if he did not know what had happened to the things that were missing, we should file a stolen property report with the insurance company. With that remark, my brother turned a shade of white and said "Maybe I have a few of the things you are talking about. Let me call home and ask my wife". It turns out that they and my crazy aunt had already been down there and had gone on a shopping spree without me! Definitely against the Trust instructions, which states that my brother and I were supposed to choose each item one by one. I insisted that the items be returned so that everything could be put in inventory, and then divided up according to the Trust.

Sickened by my brother's greed and sense of entitlement, in addition to the $300,000 that he had already embezzled, enough was enough as far as I was concerned. I decided to fight to the death for every item. I didn't care how long, or how much of a pain it was: I was damned if this insect was taking any more. I needed some bug spray to put him at bay, and asking for everything was it.

Aside from the couch, everything he wanted I said I wanted. It got right down to the pots and pans. I knew his daughter wanted them, but I had a daughter too. It was tit for tat. I was not going to budge on anything. This went on for two days. By the time it was over, I felt like I needed a vacation, as it was complete BRAIN DAMAGE.

Was it WORTH IT? Probably not, but my emotions were getting the best of me. I kept telling myself that I was almost at the finish line. I felt like I was a soldier in World War I and I was being bombed with shells: one hit me in the shoulder, then one hit me in the leg, then finally I took a bad hit to the stomach, but I was going to survive the war, NO MATTER WHAT.

I found out that this kind of behavior was more the norm than the exception. My friend Andrea went through the same thing. Her mother's will specifically stated that the household "stuff", including her personal things, would be split evenly three ways. Her sister, who was the executor, called her at the very last minute, and told her that she was at the house with her other sister dividing up the things. If she wanted anything, she had to come IMMEDIATELY. She dropped everything she was doing, and got there a couple of hours later. When she walked through the house she realized that her sister, "The Executor" had already been giving away things. Every time she asked her about some item, it was already SPOKEN FOR. When she asked for a crystal vase that she always admired, she was told that THEY had decided to give it to someone else. For the first time, she felt like she saw a new side of her two sisters. The weird thing, she thought, was that when her mom was alive, they had ALWAYS been a very close family, and had ALWAYS BEEN THERE FOR EACH OTHER. Not any more: the sisters then had a huge fight, and all that she ended up getting of her mother's possessions was a beat up chair and her mother's wedding dress. It's not a surprise that she doesn't talk to either of her sisters anymore.

When it comes to dividing up possessions, it's not just family greed that you're dealing with: it's also the other vultures that gather after someone dies. I remember when my grandfather died, all of his neighbors milled around his trailer home while we were loading the truck with his antique furniture. Each time we brought out another antique, the neighbors' eyes got bigger and bigger. The neighbors made comments like "If you don't have room for that, I can take it off your hands". Oh yeah, right, like I'm just going to hand them over a valuable antique for the hell of it! I think not. Later, a group of antique dealer vultures even came by, and said "Hi there--would you like to sell any of your furniture?" Of course, they were willing to offer us nothing for it. By the time the truck was loaded, the group of "looky-loos" were disappointed. No goodies for them. Moral of the story: beware of KIND NEIGHBORS who are not so KIND, and really watch out for the sleazy antique dealers.

It gets even more complicated when it comes to second families and second wives and husbands. My friend Francesca is a second wife, who became a widow all-to-soon. She married a generous, kind-hearted guy who thought of EVERYONE but himself, and this reflected in his trust and who got what after he died. He REALLY thought of everyone, even his friend who sold him insurance from time to time. He remembered that his friend admired his motorcycle, and he thoughtfully left it to him in his will. Francesca honored her husband's wishes after he died and gave the motorcycle to the friend. The friend asked her if he could get money from her instead, and SHE could keep the bike, as he was in dire need of cash. She told him that if he didn't want the bike, he didn't have to take it. He took the bike, and two weeks later claimed that the bike had a gas leak after he took it for a ride, and ended up burning down his garage! Being an insurance adjuster, he knew how to work the system. He even tried to sue her for giving him a motorcycle with a gas leak to the tune of $250,000 in damages! Some "friend". People can really suck at times.

Aside from the story about the motorcycle, most of these horror stories could have been avoided if only the parents and siblings had communicated while the parents were alive. A note to all of you Baby Boomers out there: COMMUNICATE WITH YOUR FAMILY. I can't stress this one element enough. Don't do like my family did. While you are still alive and of sound mind, gather your family members together and have a conversation. Videotape it as well. If you can't do that, at least put stickers on all of your items with family member's names so that they know who gets what. I had an aunt who did that, and at the time I thought she was crazy. Now I get it. Discuss who is going to get what, and WHY.

Chapter Twelve

Congratulations—You Survived!

You are now on the other side of it. When you started to read this book, you were probably confused, angry, and didn't know what the hell to do with your aging parents and dysfunctional family members. You really didn't know your parents or family at all, and your relationships with them were just illusions, at best. Before all of this happened, you had fantasies of what your family was really like. You hardly ever dealt with them, maybe on the occasional holiday or two, and everything was very superficial and nice-nice, like the pink frosting on the birthday cakes you had when you were a kid. When you cut into this cake, it wasn't up to your expectations, however. Far from it. You discovered that the cake wasn't very sweet at all. You knew something was wrong, but you just couldn't pinpoint what it was. The dynamics of your family had changed. You probably saw RED FLAGS in your parent's and sibling's behavior, but you didn't know how to deal with them. Maybe you thought to yourself "Why are my parents acting so distant from me?" RED FLAG. Reason: your sibling might be turning them against you. "Why are my parents always calling me complaining about my brother?" RED FLAG. Reason: he is asking for money all the time and might be liquidating their assets. "Why doesn't my parent's lawyer or financial advisor return my emails and phone calls?" RED FLAG. Reason: he probably has embezzled all of their money, and liquidated your inheritance. And "Why is there furniture missing from my parent's house? RED FLAG: The "oh so kind" neighbors walked off with it!

Whatever the case, when you began your journey, you faced overwhelming obstacles. No matter how much you didn't want to, you knew you had to DEAL.

By all means, YOU ARE NOT ALONE. What you are going through is an epidemic in this country. With the recession, heavy debts, and very little money to be had, millions of Baby Boomers are fighting over the scraps of money left in their parent's estates. There are so many vultures after money that you have to be conscious of them and VIGILANT. The vultures appear in many forms: overly nice next door neighbors, do-gooder attorneys, televangelists, realtors, and the one that you are really caught off guard with—your siblings.

The parents that you once knew, who were strong and vibrant people, now are senile, sickly and may even have Alzheimer's. You are the adult, taking care of them now. That means making every decision for them, whether they like it or not.

When it comes to your siblings, don't expect them to be HONEST OR FAIR. Because when it comes to money, ALL BETS ARE OFF.

Sooner or later you will be facing lawyers and trust issues. This will be very expensive, time consuming and will test your patience to the bitter end. You have to be precise and organized. It will be the small details and agreements done in writing that will be scrutinized in court or arbitration, if it goes that far. No oral agreements or handshakes will count. EVERYTHING MUST BE IN WRITING, AND NOTARIZED, IF POSSIBLE. Again, I can't stress enough that you communicate with your family members and parents while they are alive and of sound mind. Instead of superficial family gatherings where nothing of importance is discussed, your family needs to get together and discuss what is going to happen when your aging parents die, or even worse, get Alzheimer's. As I said before, I do not want what happened to me to happen to you. I don't want you writing a book like this because you went through what my family did. What I wish I had done was asked my father questions about his trust on video while he was still lucid enough to answer questions. If you can, it is essential that you videotape your parent's wishes on video. When interviewing your parents, here is a list of essential information you need:

- Make sure your parents state that they approve of the video as documentation of their wishes in addition to the written trust.

- Have them state their names, their age, and the

date that you are videotaping.

• Ask them how they feel about their mental and physical state at the time you are videotaping them.

• Ask them how they want to be buried or cremated.

• Ask them who's going to be trustees and beneficiaries of the estate.

• Ask them who's going to be executor of the estate, if any.

• If they want to exclude any family member from their estate, they must explain why so that there will be no confusion in the future.

• Ask them who has medical power of attorney.

• Ask them how they want their assets distributed.

• Ask them who gets what of the personal belongings.

• Make a copy for every family member, so no one has any question about your parent's intentions.

• As your parents get older, update your copies, as you may need to videotape them to show their deterioration of mental capacity. This could be very useful in a "testamentary capacity" case.

You may have even more questions that you want them to answer in the videotape. Be as detailed as possible to avoid misinterpretation if it comes to a court case. If they resist doing this, do whatever it takes to make this happen. Threaten them with no more holiday visits, seeing the grandkids, or NO MORE COMMUNICATION! I know that it sounds harsh, but again, DO WHATEVER IT TAKES! You must be the adult here, and you will be very, very happy that you did this. I GUARANTEE IT. If I had done this with my family, I wouldn't be out $300,000. It would have eliminated most of the vultures that came in for the kill when my dad had Alzheimer's. With this video, in addition to the trust, there will be NO DEBATES: a video is worth a thousand words, or in the case of an inheritance, maybe even millions of dollars.

Tolstoy said "Where there is law, there is injustice". This is true in the case of family trust law. Some of the laws are old, antiquated and have no bearing on today's society, as they are based on English laws written over two hundred years ago. Over the years, attorneys have found loopholes and gaps in these laws in order to have rightful heirs cheated from their legacy. The laws regarding "testamentary capacity" are the biggest offenders in trust cases. The idea that a person can be lucid for one moment, and completely crazy for the rest of the day makes absolutely no sense, BUT IT IS THE LAW. Think about it—what are the chances that a person who is demented has ONE LUCID MOMENT, lucid enough to sign an amendment to a trust that only an attorney can understand? Zero. BUT IT IS THE LAW. Why isn't anyone doing anything about this toxic law? The attorneys aren't doing anything about it because the cases take forever to try and they make a lot of money on them.

The ordinary person like you and I are not objecting loudly enough and crying out for reform. We need to write our congressmen and senators and have them address this issue. There are literally BILLIONS of dollars at stake.

Your hair might be a little grayer, and you may have a lot more wrinkles, BUT YOU SURVIVED! Fear not—a visit to the plastic surgeon, your hairdresser and a good spa vacation will revitalize you! Indulge yourself. You deserve it. Looking great and feeling great is the best revenge. You've come out of this miserable experience a much stronger person.

I had a friend who was a Vietnam vet who had a cigarette lighter that said: "Yea, though I walk through the valley of death I fear not, BECAUSE I'M THE MEANEST SONOFABITCH IN THE VALLEY!" You had no options but to be tough and endure it. THE WAR IS OVER.

ABOUT THE AUTHOR

Katherine Steel is one of the huge populace of Baby Boomers who have been left dealing with toxic inheritance and family trust problems after the death of her parents. She has written this book for all of you that have aging parents, dysfunctional siblings and bad attorneys. She wants you to spot the problems now, and fix them so that you won't go through what she did. She fervently feels that it's time for the "good kids" who didn't ask much from their parents to get smart, and get REVENGE on their scheming siblings.

www.ingramcontent.com/pod-product-compliance
Lightning Source LLC
Chambersburg PA
CBHW071703040426
42446CB00011B/1884